Patients I Will Never FORGET

SALLY WILLARD BURBANK, MD

Clovercroft Publishing

Patients I Will Never Forget

© 2014 by Sally Willard Burbank, MD

Published by Clovercroft Publishing, Franklin, Tennessee

Published in association with Larry Carpenter of Christian Book Services, LLC
www.christianbookservices.com

Cover and Interior Design by Suzanne Lawing

Edited by Lorraine Bossé-Smith

Copy Edited by Gail Fallen

Printed in the United States of America

978-1-940262-35-2

Contents

Early Years in Practice

Marriage, Motherhood & Medicine

Patients Who Inspired Me

The Fascinating, Infuriating, and Downright Scary

What About Bob?

Miracles and Divine Intervention

Patients Who Made Me Laugh

Honesty: An Overrated Virtue

Bizarre

Pregnancy and the Lack Thereof

Outrageous and More Outrageous!

Dedication

Preface

In twenty-five years of practicing primary care medicine, I have enjoyed meeting and treating thousands of patients. Some patients so inspired, maddened, or humored me, I crafted their story into a blog and then into a book. To preserve patient confidentiality, I have changed all names, ages, occupations, and other distinguishing features, and have obtained the permission of every living patient I could track down. While I have changed the details to stay in compliance with federal privacy laws (HIPAA), the gist of every story is true. Some stories are so outlandish you'll struggle to believe I didn't make them up, but I assure you, I am not that clever or creative. I hope you derive as much pleasure and inspiration from these amazing patients as I have!

Life Before
Medical
School

The Dastardly Doll that Lead Me to Medical School

I'll never forget the Christmas I discovered my bent toward science. I was six years old and huddled around the Christmas tree with my family and grandparents, anxiously waiting my turn to open a gift. My fifteen-year-old brother unwrapped and displayed the mother lode of wonderful gifts: a chemistry kit. Tiny glass bottles of cobalt blue, canary yellow, and burgundy powders mesmerized me. By adding just two drops of a magic liquid to a test tube, he could change the pH (whatever that was) and the  color of his solvent (what a wonderfully scientific sounding word) from blue to pink. How cool was that? When he heated sulfur in an Erlenmeyer flask with his Bunsen burner, the stench of rotten eggs steamed up like a poisonous brew from a witch's cauldron. I turned as green with envy as the malachite coasters my mother unwrapped.

I nearly peed my pants in anticipation while waiting for my older siblings to open their gifts. People claim the youngest child—the baby—is always spoiled rotten. For once, I would embrace the insulting stereotype if it would grant me a Christmas gift even better than my brother's. *How about a whole chemistry lab?*

Finally, my grandparents decided to torture me no longer and handed me a beautifully wrapped gift adorned with a festive red ribbon and bow. The box was so tall it came clear up to my waist. I couldn't rip the paper off fast enough. What would it be?

I yanked off the last remnant of wrapping paper and wanted to sob. Staring me in the face was a huge curly-haired baby doll. Eeww! When would people learn not all six-year-old girls want a GOOD-FOR-NOTHING, **STUPID DOLL!!!**

Of course, since I was a well-mannered six-year-old who had been taught by her mother to grin and fake gratitude over loser gifts, I pasted a half-smile on my face, stared at my shoes, and muttered, "Thank you, Grandma and Grandpa."

Despite my attempts to feign enthusiasm, my grandmother could tell I was sorely disappointed. She insisted on demonstrating all of "Betsy's" wonderful attributes. First, the silly hunk of plastic could walk. Grandma strolled Betsy across the room by pushing on her legs to-and-fro. Big deal. I could stroll across the room, and no one was flipping cartwheels over me!

My mother, now mortified over my lackluster response to the dud gift, tried to win me over by showing me Betsy's next winsome feature: she had a mouth into which I could feed water with a toy baby bottle. Mom and Grandma forced me to hold the wretched thing in my lap and tip the bottle into her mouth. Next thing I knew, my entire lap was soaking wet. Oh yes, they had neglected to inform me of Betsy's most endearing feature—she peed. All over my clothes, no less! I jumped up, horrified. Why would they give me a gift that urinated on me?

Mom and Grandma then pulled out the package of doll diapers I could have fun changing. Eeww! Doll pee? I needed every drop of maturity I possessed not to fling the vulgar creature clear across the room! What possessed my grandparents to waste hard-earned money on this horrible, no-good gift? Why did they think I'd want to change dirty diapers when I could be scheming up explosions and bubbling brews with my brother's Bunsen burner?

I excused myself under the guise of needing to change clothes, thanks to Betsy, but really, I wanted to bawl my eyes out. Oh, I forgot to mention, the dumb doll could cry tears along with me if I pushed on a certain button.

Later that day, my grandparents wanted a picture of their four grandchildren holding their Christmas gifts. Alan proudly displayed his chemistry kit; Larry, his new checker board; Ann, her paint-by-number kit; and me, my stupid, peeing doll held as far away from my body as my chubby arms could hold it.

My parents concluded that day a career in science, not daycare, was my calling.

"The Ugly Duckling is not about turning into a beautiful Barbie doll or becoming what you dream of being; It's about self-revelation and becoming who you already are."

~ Baz Luhrmann

The *Horrid Haircut* that Got Me into Med School

With the exception of gym class (who needs to know how to hit a Wiffle ball, anyhow?), school was a breeze. After graduating summa cum laude from college, I applied to medical school, a pipedream for a poor farmer's daughter like me. Nevertheless, I figured the worst they could do was turn me down and insist I never, ever apply again, right?

After mailing the all-important application, I nibbled my nails to their nubs waiting for a reply. Finally, after three tortuous months, the letter arrived. I held my breath and rip, rip, ripped open the all-important envelope that held my destiny in its ink. I skimmed the letter and jumped for joy—sort of. I had surpassed all academic requirements. Now they wanted to interview me.

While I was delighted they hadn't turned me down flat, it also meant my future lay in a thirty-minute interview with a stodgy admissions committee.

I practiced my responses to the usual questions: "Why do you want to be a doctor?" "I want to help people" was as expected an answer as was "world peace" in

"It's difficult to establish pain and suffering based on a bad hair day."

a Miss America pageant. "What is your favorite book?" *Anna Karenina*, a Russian classic by Tolstoy, ought to sound impressive. Plus, I'd actually read it.

My biggest fear was some bizarre question catching me off guard. Unfortunately, when I get nervous, instead of clamming up like normal people, I get diarrhea of the mouth; I'm bound to babble most anything, often things I wish remained unsaid. Thus, four years of grueling study could be flushed down the toilet in thirty minutes flat.

Then I was concerned about my appearance. An outdoorsy sort, I barely owned, let alone wore, makeup, and the few times I'd tried to apply it, I ended up looking like a raccoon with lipstick. I needed to exude a confident, professional (and after watching *Legally Blond*, pretty wouldn't hurt) demeanor.

I stared in the mirror and unfortunately eyed a cross between a Shih Tzu and a sheepdog staring back at me. No doubt about it—a haircut was in order. Therein lay the problem; I could barely afford my rent, let alone a fancy hair stylist. I had always gone to a local beauty school and obtained a surprisingly decent cut for dirt-cheap. Since the teachers hovered over their students like mosquitoes at a picnic and then tidied up the haircuts themselves before allowing the clients to leave, I'd always come out with an acceptable haircut, and at five dollars, it was a bargain. Plus it helped train cosmetology students. I called my usual beauty school to make an appointment, but they were completely booked. I called the alternative beauty school in town, and they could fit me right in. That should have been my red flag, but I foolishly thought, "Aren't all beauty schools the same?"

A grumpy receptionist handed me a two-page form to read and sign. I laughed aloud when I read the statements: "I understand and accept my haircut is performed by students and not licensed professionals. By signing this agreement, I abdicate the right to sue the student or the school if the haircut is deemed unacceptable."

Sue the school? Over a silly haircut? I snickered, shaking my head. Surely this was just a formality. I signed the form still chuckling.

An attendant escorted me back to the swivel chair. One look at the student assigned to me, and I wanted to dive out the nearest window. Dressed in black leather, she sported heavy chain necklaces and more piercings in her ears than I have fingers. Her persona looked more appropriate for a heavy-metal rock band than a school of cosmetology. I stared at her blue-streaked punk hair sticking up every which way and prayed she knew what the word professional meant. I scolded myself for my prudery and prejudice. Just because she looked like a freak didn't mean she couldn't cut hair, right?

Unlike the other school, where the student had to first draw a picture of the cut and then describe to the instructor in detail exactly how she planned to achieve it, this school just let the student have at it. "Danger, danger, Will Robinson!"

I informed the student I wanted a cut like Dorothy Hamill, the Olympic figure skater. She furrowed her over-pierced eyebrows and said, "Dorothy who?"

Swell! I described the stacked wedge cut popular at the time. The girl began to cut—let me rephrase that—hack at my hair like Paul Bunyan with an axe. Since the school conveniently provided no large mirrors at the stylist's station for me to inspect what she was up to, I had no idea of the disaster underway until her instructor moseyed over and screamed, "What have you done? That looks terrible! Terrible!" She flipped my hair up in disgust. "What on earth were you trying to do?"

"A D-dorothy H-hamill c-c-cut," the student stammered, shamefaced and shaking.

The instructor shook her head scowling. "That's not a Dorothy Hamill cut. Not even close." She circled around me like a vulture eyeing for road kill. She flung up my hair—what little was left—and said, as though I were as deaf as a wig on a mannequin, "I can't do anything to fix this. Not a thing! You've completely ruined her hair, and she'll just have to let it grow." She stomped away leaving both the student and me in tears.

I grabbed a mirror out of my purse and inspected the damage. My mouth dropped in horror. The back was only four inches long, and the bangs were so short and uneven they looked like a kindergartener had cut them with hedge clippers. Blindfolded. I wanted to crawl down the sink drain and bawl over my butchered tresses. Even Peter Pan had a more feminine cut. The first

thought that crossed my mind? *I want to sue this place! I'll never get into medical school looking like this.*

First impressions were so important. How could I show up for a medical school interview looking like my head had fallen into a corn auger?

Perhaps I could sport a colorful scarf on my head—the gypsy look. Alas, I did not own any festive scarves nor did I have the money to buy one, so that idea was out. If I knew a Muslim woman, I could show up in a borrowed burqa and hijab and claim I'd recently converted to Islam. That would also conveniently solve the makeup ineptitude issue. Only problem? I'd written on my application I wanted to use my future medical expertise to go on Christian medical mission trips. Thus, I would appear flaky or unbalanced to have suddenly converted to Islam. They might worry I'd next explore Hare Krishna and show up bald. No, I'd simply have to show up for the interview and hope my appearance didn't knock me out of contention for the coveted medical school slot.

As I sat down with the committee, I immediately felt eight eyeballs staring at my mutilated hair. I decided to be upfront with them. That way, they'd at least know I hadn't willingly chosen to show up for the interview looking like a savage tribe had scalped me.

I ended up entertaining the committee with my exaggerated rendition of the story. After hours of interviewing other potential students with the same dullsville question, "Why do you want to be a doctor?" they no doubt appreciated a little humor. In fact, at the end of my interview, one committee member said, "Medical school will present many challenges. You have shown us you can handle disappointment and disaster with humor and strength."

You mean my horrid haircut *helped* get me into medical school? Maybe I wouldn't sue that cosmetology school after all.

"Beware of the young doctor and the old barber."

~ BEN FRANKLIN

Medical
School

A *Psychopath* or a First-Year Medical Student?

Thanks to my dreadful haircut, I was accepted into medical school. As a Christian girl who had attended a Christian college, I was far more naïve than most twenty-two-year-olds. Truth be told, I had never seen a naked man. Thus, I was in for an "education" when I met my cadaver in my Human Anatomy class.

Five medical students were assigned to each cadaver, and I was the only woman in our group. The guys in my group affectionately named our cadaver "Fred" and were told by our instructor to keep his face and genitals covered out of respect for the dead. Hmm . . . but hacking into his chest with a buzz saw was not deemed disrespectful?

I felt like a psychopath, handling his heart and lungs late at night with no one else around. Being in a room full of dead bodies gave me the heebie-jeebies! All I needed was a pipe organ blasting a spooky rendition of Bach's *Toccata and Fugue in D minor* to thoroughly freak me out.

©2010 MARK PARISI DIST. BY UFS INC. offthemark.com

MARK PARISI

MICHAEL DISCOVERS THAT A CANTALOUPE IS ACTUALLY MUCH MORE EFFECTIVE AT KEEPING THE DOCTOR AWAY

After two weeks of dissecting, memorizing, and dreaming about the muscles, nerves, and arteries of the arm, I felt well prepared for my exam on the upper extremity. In fact, I concluded I was spending a little too much time in the cadaver room with Fred when one day, while walking downtown with my brother, we passed a muscular man in a tank top, and I couldn't help but comment, "I can picture that guy all cut up." His arm muscle definition was so distinct: biceps, triceps, deltoid, and brachioradialis, that it reminded me of my cadaver dissection.

My brother's eyes bulged, horrified and concerned. "What?" Worry etched his brow. "I think you've been breathing in too much formaldehyde." Then, thinking I'd cracked from the stress of medical school, he added, "Maybe you should see a psychiatrist or a counselor. Normal people don't want to cut up strangers on the street."

I laughed and reassured him I had merely noticed the man's distinct musculature and had no sinister plans to cut him up and stash him in the freezer.

"All work and no play make Jack a dull boy."

~ JAMES HOWELL

A Cadaver Named Fred

I was pleased when I aced my "arm" exam, but now came the awkward day when we'd remove Fred's "loin cloth" and dissect his family jewels. A fellow student flung off the covering from Fred's genitals with a flick of his arm and a dramatic "Dah-da-da-dah!"

I couldn't help but stare in horror at the nearly foot-long, three-inch wide penis. Good Lord! If all men were this big, I'd better purchase a chastity belt. Or better yet, join a convent. I whispered discretely to my anatomy partner, "Are all men that big?"

He elbowed the other men in our group and before long, they were all laughing and rolling on the floor. *What was so funny?* He finally clued me in: "I'm afraid Fred is so pumped full of

"Actually, you're my **second** patient
if you count that cadaver in med school."

formaldehyde he leaves the rest of us men feeling mighty inadequate." Turns out, Fred was *more than twice the size* of any normal man because of the embalming fluids. I felt my face flush crimson. From then on, my anatomy group teased me that my future husband would be a sore disappointment now that I had exposure to Fred.

Next we moved on to the abdomen where I quickly learned why the course was called "Gross" Human Anatomy. Since Fred was morbidly obese, we had to slice through thick layers of jiggly, bright yellow blubber. Yuck! All of us vowed to join Weight Watchers, even if we weren't fat. The mounds of fat flopped in our hands like blobs of Jell-O. It's a wonder medical students don't all develop anorexia nervosa. I did lose five pounds during the abdomen unit; Anatomy class was scheduled right before lunch.

"It is better to remain silent and be thought a fool than to open one's mouth and remove all doubt."

~ MARK TWAIN

Playing Doctor

Somehow I survived Human Anatomy without murdering a weight lifter, joining a convent, or developing an eating disorder. Next on the docket? Physical examination skills. We practiced examining each other's ears and eyes with an otoopthamalscope, and we listened to the lub-dub of each other's hearts.

Then the instructor spewed out words that nearly sent me to the admissions office to quit medical school. He wanted the female students—a decided minority of the class in 1983—to bare their chests for the male students to practice breast examination skills. *Was he crazy?* What would my boyfriend think if he knew I had allowed six classmates to grope my breasts when I wouldn't allow him to? Did this instructor think I would want the same guys I'd cut up Fred with to ogle and paw my breasts under the guise of learning physical examination skills? The guys would no doubt picture me topless from that day forward. *No way, Jose! Or William. Or Ben!* Besides, if I were inclined to flaunt my wares, which I wasn't, I'd do it at a stripper bar for

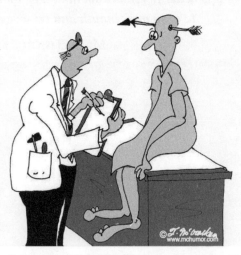

"OFF HAND, I'D SAY YOU'RE SUFFERING FROM AN ARROW THROUGH YOUR HEAD, BUT JUST TO PLAY IT SAFE, I'M ORDERING A BUNCH OF TESTS."

generous tips—I needed the money to cover medical school tuition!

The instructor tried to shame us women into compliance. "Now, women; we are all adults here. Professionals. The men will examine your breasts as just another part of your anatomy, like your eyes and ears. Right, men?"

Right, indeed! From the smirks and elbowing around the room, I concluded the instructor was delusional. Maybe the older, married students could detach enough to perceive my breasts as just another body part, but unmarried guys in their early twenties? I may be naïve, but I wasn't stupid.

Thankfully, I wasn't the only prude in the class who refused to bare her chest. Unfortunately, that forced the eight or nine willing women to be guinea pigs for the entire class. I felt guilty that these poor women were forced to endure breast exams by over a dozen men. Guilty, but not enough to volunteer.

A week later, we moved on to male anatomy. Now the tables had turned so we women could examine their goods. Amazingly, the men seemed much more willing to flaunt their family jewels than we women.

I was assigned to complete a penis and testes exam on a Middle Eastern classmate. He dropped his drawers, and my mouth dropped in shock. I found myself staring. Just my luck to get a guy with mutilated genitals. This guy's penis didn't look a thing like Fred's. Had my classmate's genitals been maimed in a war and all that remained was a blob of hanging skin? Poor fellow!

My classmate, sensing my confusion, pulled back the foreskin of his uncircumcised penis, and lo and behold, underneath all the hanging flesh was a normal looking penis. Since I had only seen the penises of Fred and a few circumcised baby boys I'd babysat, I'd never seen an uncircumcised penis before. Yet again, I felt like a fool.

I don't know which of us was more mortified. Somehow we

limped through the exam (pardon the pun), both of us avoiding eye contact at all costs. Thank God we were moving onto reflexes!

> *"Let's play doctor!" a kid said to his friend.*
>
> *"Good idea," said the other. "You operate, and I'll sue."*
>
> ~ AUTHOR UNKNOWN

The *Most Popular* Doctor in Town

I wasn't the only medical student mortified while learning physical exam skills. A male colleague may have inadvertently learned more about pleasuring a sexual partner than about proper pelvic exam technique while performing his first female exam.

Thankfully, the school knew better than to expect female medical students to guinea pig their genitals for the fumbling attempts of fellow students. Thus, they *hired* brave women to allow us newbies to practice our Pap smears and pelvic exams. The women were told in advance to provide feedback so we students could learn if we were pushing too hard or using too large a speculum.

My friend, Jeremy, wanted to become an Ob-Gyn, and he knew a gentle but thorough pelvic exam was critical to his success. Intent on perfecting his skills, he repeated the exam several times. Just when he thought he'd mastered it, his patient cooed, "Oooo, honey, keep that up, and I'm gonna have to bring you home with me."

He yanked his hands away as though her genitals were made of sulfuric acid. His face flushed redder than the body parts he'd been examining.

The woman, an audacious stand-up comedian by profession, released a bawdy laugh and waved a hand at him. "Honey, you'll be the most popular doctor in town."

About now, Jeremy wanted to dive into the dirty gown hamper and burrow deep.

She smirked. "Oh don't go getting all embarrassed on me. I just thought you ought to know before some prude files a complaint with the State Board for inappropriate sexual conduct."

SALLY WILLARD BURBANK, MD

His eyes dilated in horror. *Complaint with the State Board? Inappropriate sexual conduct?* Maybe he should switch his specialty to general surgery.

She punched his arm. "Hey, cheer up. If you ever decide this doctoring thing ain't your cup of tea, you'd make a marvelous gigolo." She released another raucous laugh and added, "Honey, you ever need someone to practice on, give me a call." She then burst into boisterous laughter, amused at her own humor.

Jeremy, however, was not amused. Where had the school found this woman? A brothel?

Of course, from that day forward, Jeremy endured endless razzing about his special touch. What a delightful change for someone else to occupy the laughingstock chair for once, but not for long . . .

"Bedside manners are no substitute for the right diagnosis."

~ **ALFRED P. SLOAN**

Old Faithful and *Me*

Of the endless opportunities medical school provided to embarrass myself, learning to draw blood and start IVs were the worst offenders. I blamed my eyes' lack of depth perception, but for weeks, I was so inept I'd probably have failed to tap oil from the Alaska pipeline. In fact, I couldn't tell you who dreaded my futile attempts more—the patient or me.

One day, my humiliation reached a new peak. I mashed my shaky index finger on the inner elbow of a patient to whom I'd been assigned to obtain three vials of blood. I couldn't feel a thing that felt like a plump vein. The two blood-drawing failures earlier that day had done little to bolster my confidence that I would ever obtain a drop—let alone three vials—from the bruised arm perched in front of me.

The patient eyed me suspiciously, no doubt sensing my insecurity. "You ever done this before?"

"Yes, I'm highly skilled at drawing blood. I never miss."

I knew if I told her "not successfully," she'd kick me out of her hospital room immediately, and my senior resident had been adamant: "Do not leave her room until you have three full tubes of blood." Thus, I couldn't tell her I had poked and prodded many patients but had never successfully obtained blood, or she'd threaten me with a lawsuit if I mutilated her veins. I responded with as much confidence as I could muster, "Oh, I've stuck needles in lots of patients before." I left out the minor detail how said needles had never actually retrieved any blood.

My heart thudded in panic as I applied the tourniquet and probed each of her elbow bends, desperate to find a plump, untapped vein. I touched what I thought was my best bet, hurled a hasty prayer toward heaven, and jabbed the needle in as delicately and quickly as I could. Wonder of wonders, miracle of miracles, I actually penetrated a vein, and the red liquid of life flowed into the tube. Once I had filled all three tubes, I was so ecstatic about my first successful phlebotomy that I pulled the needle out of her arm before first removing the tourniquet. Before I could mutter, "Whoops," a geyser of blood spurted straight toward the ceiling, landing on my patient's head, clothes, and face. Blood splattered all over my white lab coat.

I quickly tugged off the tourniquet and mashed a cotton ball to her arm, my face now redder than the blood dripping off her bedrail. I wanted to slither into the tube of blood and swim out of sight. No way would I look this lady in the eyes.

But the next thing I knew, she was laughing! "What'd you do, hit my aorta?" she asked, mopping the blood off her face. "Too bad that wasn't oil you struck—we'd both be rich."

As I cleaned up the mess she added, "If things don't work out with medical school, perhaps you could get a job at Yellowstone." We shared a chuckle about Old Faithful, and then I escaped with the proof of my first successful phlebotomy.

Well—sort of successful.

That night I uttered a special prayer for the kind lady with a sense of humor and a tolerance for inept medical students.

With more practice, I eventually mastered blood drawing, but my skills at starting IVs remained atrocious. Good thing medical students were unpaid, or I'd have been fired.

> *"The tongue, like a sharp knife,*
> *can kill without drawing blood."*
>
> ~ BUDDHA

A Lesson Learned the Hard Way

During my fourth year of medical school, I completed an acting internship at a Veterans Administration (VA) hospital. Because the VA hospital was often chronically short-staffed, medical students and interns were treated like slave labor; we were responsible for drawing all the blood and starting all the IVs. Thus, working twenty-hour shifts without a single break were not uncommon.

After one particularly draining night, I crawled into bed at three in the morning, exhausted and cranky. I'd worked at a frenetic pace since seven the previous morning and hadn't even had time to eat supper. My stomach grumbled in protest, but if given a choice between sleep and food, even I, a card-carrying foodaholic, chose sleep. Just then, my beeper buzzed.

With squinty eyes, I glanced at my beeper and suppressed a curse—Nurse Ratchet at the Zoo. The "Zoo" was the term we interns used for the poverty ward where a dozen patient beds were lined up like cribs in a Soviet orphanage. Nurse Ratchet, the battle-ax head nurse, despised interns even more than her patients.

I called her back with as pleasant a voice as I could muster at three in the morning when dog tired, and Nurse Ratchet informed me I needed to come start an IV on Horace Green. I dragged myself out of bed, stretched, and plodded toward the Zoo. I dreaded my upcoming task, as I would no doubt have to poke and prod his arms for thirty minutes before finally achieving a functioning IV. Meanwhile, Nurse Ratchet would stand over my shoulder either sneering or snickering at my failed attempts. My hands would shake worse than an epileptic fit.

I trudged into the ward and located Mr. Green's name at the bottom of his bed and then began the first of six attempts to start his IV. Both of his arms already bore the splotchy, swollen, black, blue, green, and yellow evidence of previous incompetent medical student phlebotomy attempts. Every good vein—from his shoulders to his fingernails—had already been blown or butchered. Thankfully, he was so gorked out on pain medication that he didn't even flinch at my fumbling attempts. Final-ly, on the sixth try, I accomplished my goal. I connected the IV to a bag of saline. Thank goodness Nurse Ratchet was nowhere in sight and hadn't tapped her foot impatiently the whole time.

I yawned and plodded back to bed, praying I could get at least three hours of sleep before morning rounds. I had bare-ly flopped my bedraggled body onto the paper-thin, sagging mattress before my pager beeped again. I wanted to clobber my cheapo mattress with a club, but hadn't the strength or energy to do so. I glanced at my beeper and groaned—Nurse Ratchet. *Again.* WHAT DOES THE OLD BAT WANT NOW? I dialed her number, and she snapped, "I thought I told you to start an IV on Horace Green. Why haven't you done it? He needs his vancomycin."

"I *did* start his IV," I said, unable to suppress my indignant tone.

"Well, I'm standing right next to his bed, and he has no IV."

Had the old codger pulled out his IV already? If so, I'd wring his neck, and he wouldn't *need* another IV! (A twenty-hour workday with no supper and no sleep had done little to sweeten my mood or bedside manner.)

I stomped back to the ward sputtering. Just as I'd said, Mr. Green lay in his bed with a fully functioning IV. *What was her problem?* Had she paged me back up here just to be mean? I charged up to Nurse Ratchet. "Why did you wake me up again? Mr. Green's IV is working perfectly."

With her hands on her hips and a condescending glint in her eyes, she said, "Afraid not."

"I'll prove it to you," I said, annoyed at her priggish tone. I marched her over to Mr. Green's bed and gestured toward his IV. "Voila, just like I said. A fully functioning IV."

Nurse Ratchet smirked. "You started an IV, all right—just not on Horace Green. That's Elmer Potts."

My mouth dropped in shock. *"What???"* I pointed to the name posted in large letters at the bottom of the bed. "It says right there—Horace Green."

In a patronizing tone, she said, "Don't they teach you interns to check armbands anymore? We have so many patients on this ward they sleep in whatever bed is vacant. Elmer must have taken Horace's bed, so Horace is sleeping over there." She pointed at another patient snoring in a nearby bed—*without* an IV.

I wanted to scream. "You mean I just wasted thirty minutes starting an IV *on the wrong patient?*"

She grinned, unable to contain her glee. "You got it. And meanwhile, Mr. Green needs his IV—just like I said."

I wanted to cram the IV pole right down her cocky gullet. That cheeky nurse derived far too much pleasure from my mistake. Her folded arms and I-told-you-so expression stuck in my craw like a chunk of spoiled scrod. However, another intern had warned me to stay on Nurse Ratchet's good side, or I would live to regret it. Since I had to work with the maddening shrew an entire month, I decided I'd better smooth things out between us. "Guess I learned *that* lesson the hard way, didn't I?" I muttered, forcing myself to smile and chuckle in feigned humor.

Luckily, she accepted my olive branch and even offered to gather the IV supplies I'd need to start an IV on the real Mr. Green.

On a positive note, never again have I performed a procedure on a patient without first checking his armband!

> *"Rough diamonds are sometimes mistaken*
> *for worthless pebbles."*
>
> ~ THOMAS BROWNE

How I Outsmarted a Pack of Ravenous Wolves

I had nearly survived my month-long acting internship at the Veterans Administration (VA) hospital under the intimidating tutelage of Nurse Ratchet. My skills at drawing blood and starting IVs had grown astronomically, and hence, the number of leers and rolled eyes I endured from the disparaging ogress had dropped precipitously. In my last week at the VA, though, an incident happened that would test our shaky truce:

Edgar Summers, a patient with severe Alzheimer's disease, was convinced wolves were prowling outside the hospital waiting for him to fall asleep so they could sneak in and gobble him up. Nurse Ratchet had already tried reasoning with him, but Edgar became more agitated and accused her of *wanting* him eaten so she could admit another patient to his room. Edgar had overheard Nurse Ratchet tell an emergency room doctor that all her beds were full so she couldn't accept more patients.

A nurse's aide tried to calm Edgar down by telling him she had sent a security officer outside to take care of the wolves. Big mistake. Now Edgar was convinced the security officer had been eaten alive. Nurse Ratchet ended up paging the security officer to Edgar's room to reassure him he was unharmed and had scared the wolves away.

Edgar insisted the wolves would soon be back. At this point, Nurse Ratchet paged me and wanted me to prescribe him a shot of Haldol, a potent anti-psychotic drug, to simmer down his

paranoia and put him to sleep.

Before resorting to sedating medications, which can increase the risk of falls and hip fractures in the elderly, I wanted to try one more non-pharmaceutical approach to rid him of his irrational phobia.

First, a word of explanation, or I'll be written off as a miserable liar:

Most people assume when an Alzheimer's patient gets confused and thinks his dead wife is alive or his daughter hasn't visited in a month—even though she came yesterday—or a pack of hungry wolves is chasing him, that they should tell the Alzheimer's patient the truth and try to convince him he is confused or just plain wrong. The problem is, this never works. It only addles and angers the patient, as it did Edgar Summers. The patient won't believe you, and even if he did, he won't remember a word you said in ten minutes. Usually, he will insist you are wrong, because in his mind, you are! Thus, the argument between the two of you becomes as productive as most congressional budget negotiations. Why? Because in the mind of the Alzheimer's patient, the dead wife is still alive, his daughter hasn't visited in a month, and ravenous wolves are hovering outside the hospital.

Thus, to calm a demented patient, instead of trying to force him back into your world aka the land of the rational and non-demented, you have to put yourself in his world, and then make it better. Thus, instead of insisting, "That's not right, Daddy. Mama died five years ago," or "No, Daddy, you're wrong. I was just here yesterday," or "No wolves are outside," the daughter (or nurse or doctor) is better off saying, "Mama made the best apple pie, didn't she, Daddy?" or "I'm so glad I came to visit you today," or "Let's figure out how we can outsmart those wolves."

While some may consider this lying, in reality, it is the only way to calm an addled and demented person. In short, when in Rome, do as the Romans do.

Thus, with this understanding of severe Alzheimer's, I sat in a chair beside Edgar's bed and told him I knew of a foolproof method to protect him and all the other patients in the hospital from the vicious wolves. I told him about the four-digit security code that had to be punched in before the doors to the hospital would open after nine o'clock at night. "Edgar," I whispered, "I'm going to change that security code to a new code the wolves don't know. Then they won't be able to get in."

His wrinkled brow furrowed. "You'll use a code the wolves don't know?"

"Exactly, and I'll even let you pick the numbers. That way, only you and I know the code."

He smiled and whispered four arbitrary numbers into my ear, relieved we had found a way to outsmart the ravenous beasts. I left the room to supposedly go change the security code. When I came back fifteen minutes later, Edgar was sound asleep. Even Nurse Ratchet was impressed.

My clever scheme worked until the next night when Edgar insisted an angry clan of rhinos would charge into the hospital using their horns to smash down the doors. Thus, even changing the security code wouldn't protect him. But that's another story . . .

"His memory is like wares at an auction—
going, going, gone."

~ HERMAN MELVILLE

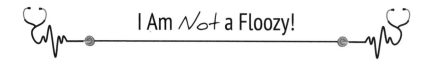

I Am Not a Floozy!

When I started medical school, I was determined to make the Alpha Omega Alpha Honor Society. Only the top 10 percent of the class was offered a spot in this coveted group, and unbeknownst to me, every other medical student was just as competitive as I. Worse yet, medical school was nothing like high school or college, where the dumb, stoned, drunken, and lazy made staying in the top ten a breeze. On the contrary, my medical school class consisted of an intimidating posse of students with photographic memories, IQs of 160, Ivy League degrees, and rich parents. Unlike me, most didn't have to work twenty hours a week in the medical library to afford tuition. Compared to my classmates, who had inherited a genetic jackpot, for the first time in my life, no matter how much I studied, I felt mediocre. Since I had always tested near the top of my class, this drove me crazy. After all, who would choose to be Salieri when he could be Mozart?

I discovered after my first Human Anatomy test that grades were posted by name, from the top scorer to the bottom scorer, for everyone to see. I was disappointed I didn't make the top ten. In fact, I ranked number twenty-three out of one hundred medical students in the class. Not to worry, I reassured myself. Now that I was familiar with the tests, I'd study harder and bring my ranking into the top ten.

In my dreams! On test two, I ranked number eleven. Test three? Number eleven. Test four? Number eleven. No matter how much I studied, I was doomed for the lowly number-eleven spot, which came with no glory, no honors grade, and no elusive Alpha Omega Alpha Honor Society membership.

Just because I didn't qualify for Alpha Omega Alpha didn't mean I couldn't score at least one honors grade during my four years, right? After all, when the time came to apply for residency programs, an honors grade would look great on my application, and it might raise my chances of acceptance into a top program.

I loved Microbiology with all its bizarre sounding diseases: *Yersinia pestis* (bubonic plague), *Borrelia burgdorferi* (Lyme disease), and those gross worm infections where the larvae live in your lungs, then get coughed up and swallowed down into your intestines where they develop into worms that lay eggs. Somehow, I found the nasty little critters fascinating, so if I could ace any class, it would be Micro. I studied so much I was even dreaming about hookworms and slime molds.

As I sat down to my final Micro exam, I was number nine in the class. Finally! My chance to shine and capture that elusive honors grade. When the final grades were posted, I was back down to—you guessed it—number eleven. I wanted to clobber the list with a six-foot-long tapeworm. Even more maddening, the two guys who placed ninth and tenth attended my Monday-night prayer group. Guess I couldn't ask the group to pray for me to make the top ten, or we'd be praying that they didn't! Plus, I suspect God doesn't like prayers that pad MY ego rather than His kingdom. Thus, I was left still hoping to catch the elusive Loch Ness monster of medical school grades—honors.

Then one day, our Human Sexuality teacher mentioned how any student who wrote an optional twenty-page research paper on an approved topic and maintained a score of at least ninety on all tests would qualify for an honors grade. My ears perked up. I could do that. THIS was my answer to prayer—my honors grade.

I studied hard and aced the tests. I squandered dozens of hours holed up in the library researching and writing a twenty-page term paper on the "Physiological Response of the Sexual Act." Back then, we still had to use an ancient device called a typewriter, not some easy WordPerfect computer program where errors and typos could be fixed with the simple click of a mouse. And, instead of performing a simple Google search (while clad in pajamas and sipping a caramel latte in the comfort of my own home), my research involved lifting dusty medical tomes heavy enough to tear my rotator cuff from the top shelves of the library.

Since I had recently married my long-time sweetie, Nathan, I asked—all right, insisted—that he proofread my literary gem. Two hours later, bleary-eyed and yawning, he commented, "That paper sure sucks the fun out of sex."

I took it a promising sign—scholarly research was supposed to be boring, right?

When I finally received my first honors grade, I leaped around the room like Tigger on Ritalin. I waved the proof in my husband's face, waiting for his praise and adoration—something along the lines of, "I'm so lucky to be married to such a brilliant woman." Instead, he scowled and mumbled the lame comment that it had to be a mistake because if I was an honors student in sex, HE sure saw no signs of it!

Okay, true confessions: I'd been so busy studying, researching, and *writing* about sex, who had time to actually *have* any? Apparently my sex-starved husband would gladly have traded my coveted honors grade and tedious term paper for a roll in the hay. Oh well, I'd make it up to him now that I had my honors grade. After all, a little less hanky-panky was worth it if an honors grade improved my chances of snagging a top residency slot.

When the time came to apply for internships, however, I realized my fatal mistake. I now had a transcript that stated I was merely average in every subject except one: sex! In short, I looked like some nymphomaniac who'd slept with her professors to obtain a passing grade in all her other classes.

Maybe no one will notice.

Wrong! During one interview, the director perused my transcript then smirked. "I see your only honors grade was in Human Sexuality." He ogled me and frowned, as though thinking, *She doesn't* look *like she'd be any good in bed.* Talk about embarrassing!

I was greeted with the same humiliating reaction at my next two interviews. By my last interview, I was ready to wear a sandwich board stating, **"I AM NOT A FLOOZY."**

Luckily, I landed a great residency slot in Nashville *despite* graduating number eleven in the class, with no honors society membership, and with a transcript that looked more promising for a hooker than a doctor.

Three years later, I took the National Board exams. Three guesses what my national ranking was: the top *eleventh* percentile! ARGH!

"For the lips of a forbidden woman drip with honey,
and her speech is smoother than oil;
but in the end she is bitter as wormwood,
sharp as a two-edged sword."

~ Proverbs 5:3-4 (English Standard)

Internship and Residency

The Spider on the Wall

Internship and residency could be summed up in five words: all work and no play. The amount of knowledge and experience crammed into three years boggles the mind. As I was no longer a bungling maladroit, Nurse Ratchet had to find some other poor intern to torment. The tables had turned, and one day, I even got to correct Nurse Ratchet!

At age ninety, Cora Jones suffered moments when her memory failed. She'd lose her nephew's name, the gist of Sunday's sermon, if she'd eaten lunch, and what her daughter told her she wanted for Christmas. Thus, when she was admitted to the hospital for an emergency gallbladder surgery, no one was surprised when she couldn't remember the name of her blood pressure medication or her surgeon. The admitting nurse quickly concluded Cora must have early Alzheimer's and passed along her suspicion to Nurse Ratchet, who was scheduled for the night shift.

When Cora pushed the nurse button to report a huge spider crawling on the ceiling above her bed, Nurse Ratchet didn't take her seriously. The woman was obviously sun downing. Nurse Ratchet cranked down the morphine drip, confident that would take care of the "spider."

Thirty minutes later, Cora rattled her bed rails and mashed on the nurse button again. "I can't sleep with that spider glaring down at me. It could be a brown recluse waiting to bite me." She seemed to have no problem coming up with the name brown recluse!

Nurse Ratchet documented in the medical record that not only was Cora seeing things, she now displayed paranoia. She reassured Cora through the intercom, "There, there, dearie. There's no spider; it's just your morphine making you hallucinate." She sauntered down the hall and turned off Cora's morphine drip. She then called the surgeon requesting an antipsychotic medication to settle her down.

Cora refused to take it: "I don't need drugs! I need you to kill that spider!"

Nurse Ratchet smiled and patted her hand then quickly exited the room, refusing to validate Cora's imaginary spider by actually inspecting the walls and ceiling.

When I entered Cora's room on rounds the next morning, the first words out of her mouth? "I couldn't sleep a wink with that huge spider above my head." She crossed her arms in disgust. "That nurse didn't believe a word I said. She kept turning down my pain medication, and now I hurt so bad I can barely get out of bed. She should be fired!"

I inspected the room for a spider just to prove Cora wrong. I nearly dropped my morning coffee when, on the ceiling directly above Cora's head, WAS a large brown spider sitting in the middle of his web! Cora pointed accusingly at the arachnid. "I *told* that nurse there was a spider. She wouldn't even look!"

Imagine the delight I took in turning the tables on Nurse Ratchet and informing her of her error in judgment!

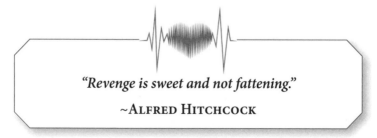

"Revenge is sweet and not fattening."

~ALFRED HITCHCOCK

A *New* Treatment for AIDS?

As interns and residents, we admitted patients from the emergency room every fourth night, and if the patient didn't have a primary care doctor, we would follow them after hospital discharge in our outpatient residents' clinic. The hospital where I trained was located in the heart of the inner city, so I was exposed to people I had never seen in the rural community in which I'd been raised. Take Marty, for example. Although he was only twenty-three years old, he arrived at the emergency room complaining of crushing chest pain that turned out to be a heart attack caused by cocaine.

Cocaine abuse wasn't the only thing that distinguished Marty from other men; he ranked as the most effeminate male I had ever encountered. His voice was a full octave higher than mine, he wore long manicured red nails, and when he walked, he sashayed his hips like a runway model. No wonder—it turned out he worked as a female impersonator at a gay strip club downtown.

I may be naive, but even I deduced he was a male prostitute. Thus, besides treating his heart attack, I ordered tests for AIDS, syphilis, gonorrhea, and every other sexually transmitted disease I could think of.

Because he had no medical insurance and couldn't afford drug rehab, we advised him to join Cocaine Anonymous. After we stabilized his heart, we discharged him with the strict instructions to stay away from cocaine, to use condoms, and to follow up with me at my outpatient medical clinic in one week.

Laboratory results returned a week later, but unfortunately, Marty did not! I glanced at the lab report, and my jaw dropped in horror when *every* single sexually transmitted disease came back positive! Since this pre-dated AZT (the first potent medication discovered to treat AIDS), I would effectively be handing him a death sentence. Plus, if he worked as a prostitute, no telling how many other men he had infected.

I notified the Health Department, but they informed me later that day that the phone number and address he'd provided to the hospital were bogus. "Typhoid Marty" was still at large and potentially infecting others. He had to be located and treated.

Desperate to track him down, I called every gay strip club in the area and finally located him. Not wanting to tell him he had AIDS over the telephone, I convinced him to come to my outpatient clinic for some "very important news."

Legs crossed like a fashion model, he sat in my exam room admiring his long manicured nails while I broke the terrible news that he had AIDS, syphilis, gonorrhea, chlamydia, herpes, and venereal crabs! I injected him with penicillin and wrote out prescriptions for all of the other treatable diseases. I then delivered a simplified dissertation on what it meant to be HIV positive with a dangerously low T4 helper count. Since condoms can break, I advised he should never have sex again or he might spread the fatal disease to others. Knowing he would be devastated, I inhaled a deep breath and said, "Do you have any questions, Marty?"

He glanced up and inquired in his delicate voice, "Will you give me estrogen?"

Puzzled, I said, "Estrogen? That won't help AIDS."

He shook his head. "That's not why I want it. I want it to make my breasts bigger."

I stared at him in shock. I'd just told him he had every venereal disease known to man and would probably die of AIDS, and all he was concerned about was the size of his breasts?

"Increasing breast size is not an FDA-approved indication for estrogen. Furthermore, it has serious risks, such as leg clots and strokes. I won't prescribe it to you."

Unfazed, he squeaked out, "Do you know any doctors who *will*?"

This encounter was not going well. I reminded myself to remain professional. I wondered how an experienced internist would handle this guy. I finally blurted out, "No ethical doctor in Nashville will prescribe estrogen just to make your breasts bigger."

Not backing down, he said, "You know any *un*ethical doctors?"

I closed my eyes, clueless as to how to respond. Medical school had not prepared me for patients like Marty. I told him I'd treat his AIDS and infectious diseases, but he'd have to locate an unethical doctor on his own!

A few months later, I noticed his breasts were indeed growing larger, so he obviously had obtained estrogen somewhere.

His immune system continued to plummet, so when azidothymidine (AZT) was released a year or two later, I was elated. I finally had something to offer my patients with AIDS.

Unfortunately, Marty was non-compliant with his AIDS medications. Judging from the size of his breasts, however, he never missed his estrogen! Not surprisingly, he died of *Pneumocystis carinii*, an AIDS-related pneumonia, four years later.

*"You can lead a horse to water,
but you can't make it drink."*

~ AUTHOR UNKNOWN

Couvade's Syndrome

One night when I was on call, Douglas, a seemingly healthy twenty-five-year-old, was admitted to the hospital with vomiting, dehydration, and obscure abdominal cramps. Initially, we thought he had picked up a simple stomach virus, but when he was still vomiting three days later, we began an exhaustive series of tests to find out what was wrong. All of the test results came back normal, and with a normal temperature and white blood count, infection seemed unlikely. In short, we were stumped.

Luckily, we solved the case three days later when his wife, who was two months pregnant, came to visit him for the first time. Turns out, she hadn't come to see him earlier because she'd been hunched over the commode vomiting her guts out with morning sickness. Doug's vomiting started shortly after his wife's morning sickness started. Of course! Doug had Couvade's syndrome.

Couvade's syndrome, also called "sympathy pregnancy," is a psychosomatic syndrome where the male partner of a pregnant woman develops the same symptoms as his wife. It can include weight gain, back pain, nausea, vomiting, and postpartum depression. The syndrome has been de-

"First step is the hardest. You've got to admit that you don't have a problem."

scribed in cultures all around the world for centuries.

As expected, Douglas made a full recovery once his wife's nausea and vomiting improved at the beginning of her fourth month.

"If nature had arranged that husbands and wives should have children alternatively, there would never be more than three in a family."

~ LAWRENCE HOUSMAN

Not Until the Priest Comes

Exposure to languages and cultures completely foreign to me proved one of the joys of interning in a city with a diverse international population. I discovered through a malaria patient from Zimbabwe, for example, that one could communicate with clicks of the tongue instead of words. The patient spoke Zulu, and his interpreter translated his various clicks and grunts into words. Another time, I stuck out a friendly hand of greeting to the son of an elderly Egyptian woman, only to discover devout Muslim men do not touch women, even if the woman is his mother's doctor. Awkward! Did I have a lot to learn.

Sometimes, even Americans from traditional religious backgrounds can display odd behaviors. Case in point: Jonathan Monroe grew up in a devout Catholic home where attending

mass every Sunday and reciting Hail Marys were as much a part of daily life as bread and potatoes.

Unfortunately, despite completing Catechism and twelve years at a parochial school, Jonathan rebelled against everything his parents, priests, and schoolteacher nuns had taught him. First, binge drinking, then marijuana, and then cocaine addiction so severe it consumed his life. Mrs. Monroe prayed the Rosary and lit candles for her prodigal son. She forked out thousands of dollars for in-patient drug rehabilitation and attended Al-Anon meetings, but all to no avail—Jonathan's addiction reigned supreme.

One fateful day, Jonathan's cocaine abuse raised his blood pressure so high, it triggered a massive stroke. His girlfriend found him hours later fully comatose and barely breathing. She summoned an ambulance and notified his parents.

Paramedics on the scene found his blood pressure a whopping 260/160, and he was unarousable. They rushed him to the hospital where an emergency CAT scan revealed the massive stroke.

By this time, his parents arrived and were understandably devastated. Mrs. Monroe could barely contain her sobbing long enough to hear the grim prognosis. "The extent of his brain injury is incompatible with life," the neurologist stated as kindly as he could. "In fact, I don't know how he's survived as long as he has."

In an effort to console Mrs. Monroe, who was clutching her son's hand, I placed a comforting hand on her heaving shoulder and said, "I'll bet Jonathan was holding on long enough for you to tell him goodbye."

She suddenly straightened up and gripped my arm. "You cannot let him die until Father Bryant gets here and performs Last Rites. It's his only hope."

No sooner were the words out of her mouth than Jonathan quit breathing altogether and went into cardio-respiratory arrest. His mother shrieked, "Do something! Do something! You cannot let him die!"

We immediately launched into CPR and hollered for the nurse to announce overhead "Code Blue, Neurointensive Care Unit." Within a minute, an entire team of nurses and doctors dashed into the room, and an endotracheal tube was inserted down his mouth and into his trachea. The nurse squeezed an Ambu bag of oxygen down the endotracheal tube to his lungs. I initiated chest percussions at a firm and rapid pace.

After an infusion of epinephrine, we stopped CPR long enough to see if he had responded. No luck. We resumed CPR, but after ten full minutes of performing the Advanced Cardiac Life Support (ACLS) protocol to the letter with no response, Jonathan was obviously dead, and nothing we did would change that.

Just as we were ready to call off the resuscitation effort and pronounce him legally dead, his mother barged into the room and insisted Jonathan would go straight to hell for all eternity if we pronounced him dead before he received Last Rites from Father Bryant. To my knowledge, this was not official Catholic doctrine, but who was I to delve into deep, theological debates in the middle of performing CPR on Jonathan's deathbed!

Thus, out of compassion for Mrs. Monroe, the neurologist insisted we resume the code. After an additional twenty minutes of performing futile chest percussions on a corpse, the neurologist glanced at his watch and inquired of Mrs. Monroe, who was standing outside the door, "Any idea when Father Bryant will make it to the hospital?"

The mother glanced over at her husband. "When did he tell you he'd be here, Harold?"

The father's head jerked up. "I didn't call him. I thought you did."

The mother looked incensed. "I didn't call him. I told you to!"

Mr. Monroe ran toward the nursing station to call Father Bryant.

The nurses and doctors on the code team all groaned. We had performed CPR with no response for thirty minutes and *the priest hadn't even been called?*

By now, the body was mottled, cold, and bloated. The shoulders of one outspoken member of the code team slumped, and he spoke what we were all thinking. "Come on! This guy is dead and has been for thirty minutes. We need to call this charade off and pronounce him dead."

Hands cramping and back aching after thirty minutes of vigorous (and futile) chest percussions, stopping sure sounded good to me! Another team member agreed. "What are we waiting for—rigor mortis?"

"The funeral?" a third team member said.

"Maggots?" piped in another.

A male nurse added, "Besides, if this dude is bound for hell, us beating on his chest another twenty minutes isn't going to make a difference. Let's call it a day."

Unfortunately, unbeknownst to us, Mrs. Monroe was still standing right outside the door and had overheard all the ghastly, irreverent comments. I'm so glad for once I'd kept my fat mouth shut! She barged into the room, tears streaming down her face, and pointed her index finger at the mouthy male nurse who muttered the dreadful comment. "So help me, I'll sue every one of you if you let him die before Father Bryant gets here."

We momentarily froze then resumed our bagging and chest percussions with renewed vigor! Jonathan? Not so much—his muscles stiffened, and his eyes stared lifelessly into space.

Finally, after a full fifty minutes of performing CPR, Father Bryant rushed into the room to perform his priestly functions. I wanted to kiss his feet and say, "Bless you, Father!" but my back was too stiff and achy to bend.

When the priest completed the Last Rites, the neurologist

officially pronounced Jonathan dead, and the whole code team collapsed in exhaustion.

That grueling hour of performing CPR on a young man dying from an overdose ranks as the most gut-wrenching hour I experienced in my three years of residency. I can only hope the Last Rites brought comfort and peace to a mother who had faced the saddest tragedy a parent can endure. She'd already faced the downward trajectory of her son's escalating drug addiction and repetitive poor choices. Tears filled my eyes at the terrible waste of a life. I couldn't help but feel the deepest compassion for Mrs. Monroe as the thought crossed my mind, "What if this had been my son?"

"The first half of our life is ruined by our parents and the second half by our children."

~ CLARENCE DARROW

"How sharper than a serpent's tooth it is to have a thankless child."

~ WILLIAM SHAKESPEARE

It's *Too Late* for Sheila

I met Sheila, a twenty-six-year-old, on the psychiatric ward where I was a clueless third-year medical student completing my three-month psychiatry rotation. Sheila was on suicide watch after a half-baked Tylenol overdose attempt. She had immediately called 911 after swallowing the pills.

Thanks to Weight Watchers, Sheila had lost sixty pounds in the previous year, but had recently regained thirty because of her binge-eating disorder. When we rounded on her each morning, Sheila parroted the same words: "I hate myself for gaining that weight back. I'm such a loser, I could kill myself."

Sheila's entire self-worth was wrapped up in one thing: a number on the scale. Since this was 1984, before the release of Prozac and Topamax and other effective medications for eating disorders and severe depression, the only drugs available had nasty side effects, including weight gain. Thus, Sheila refused to take them. Cognitive behavioral therapy had yet to be discovered.

"Try to make it more interesting than last time."

The head of the Psychiatry Department was an atheist and wouldn't even allow Bibles on the psych ward. He attempted to treat Sheila with what he called "extinguish therapy." This meant that anytime Sheila mentioned her weight, self-hatred, or a desire to kill herself, we were supposed to ignore it and immediately change the subject. If she talked about anything positive, we were supposed to reward her by staying engaged, telling her how much we enjoyed her company, and giving her attention. He claimed this would use positive reinforcement to encourage her not to dwell on her weight. I was unconvinced. I felt she was just being taught to not talk about her feelings and to hide her self-hatred from us.

Since I have always struggled with weight myself, I understood Sheila's disgust at gaining back weight she had worked so hard to lose. Though I have never been suicidal, bulimic, or prone to severe depression, I hoped by spending more time with her, I could somehow help her. I got permission to go for a one-hour walk with her each day. I told her the best thing she could do was to not focus on the past, which she could not change, but to start working on the future by slowly losing those thirty pounds. Focus on what you *can* change, I told her. Take things one day at a time, I insisted. A daily one-hour walk was a great place to start, right?

While we walked each day, Sheila seemed obsessed with self-flagellation, and all my encouraging words were ignored. As far as she was concerned, she was a worthless person because she was thirty pounds overweight. Every time she said the words, "I hate myself for gaining back that weight; I could just shoot myself," a chill ran down my spine. "Don't do that, Sheila! People love you and would be devastated if you killed yourself."

"Nobody loves me," she insisted. "Who'd love a Goodyear blimp?"

After two weeks of walking every day with Sheila, she began to open up a bit about her dysfunctional childhood and her stepfather, who had made cruel remarks about her weight on a daily basis. I now understood why she obsessed about weight as a barometer for her self-worth.

She shared her goal of one day becoming a librarian because she loved to read. I brought in several of my favorite novels and told her we'd talk about them once she finished reading them. I hoped reading would distract her from her weight obsession and give us something fresh to talk about.

On several occasions, I threw out comments how God loved her unconditionally, no matter what she weighed. He had a plan for her life, I insisted. Since the head of the Psychiatry Department had already given me an ultimatum for sharing Scripture with another suicidal Christian patient, I had to be careful how much I shared, or I could be thrown out of my psych rotation. (His exact words!)

After three weeks on the psych ward, the head of the department said Sheila was ready to go home. He claimed she was no longer ruminating about her weight and was much better.

It was audacious of me, but I told him I totally disagreed. From my daily walks with Sheila, I felt she was still suicidal and was not safe to go home. I informed him that on yesterday's walk, she'd told me, "I could shoot myself for gaining all that weight back." The psychiatrist peered over the top of his reading glasses, clearly nettled that I'd dared to challenge his judgment. In a condescending voice he inquired, "And you completed your psychiatric residency program where? You passed your Psychiatry Medical Boards, when?"

Titters erupted from the other medical students. Completely humiliated, I said no more, and Sheila was discharged against my better judgment.

But I worried about her.

I called her and walked with her as much as my schedule allowed. I even invited her to attend church with me. She said "maybe." I listened—and shared Bible verses offering hope.

One day, a week after she was discharged from the hospital, I called to check on her because she'd seemed unusually depressed on our walk the day before. Imagine my horror when her roommate informed me, "Sheila's dead. She got ahold of a gun and shot herself in the head last night."

I nearly dropped the phone. *Sheila was dead?*

My heart lurched, and I couldn't breathe. She killed herself? Twelve hours earlier, we'd walked on the shore of Lake Champlain. Now she was dead. I flopped into a chair too shocked to utter a sound.

Guilt overwhelmed me. I should have stood up to the head of Psychiatry and told him, even though I was just a lowly medical student, Sheila was NOT safe to leave the hospital. I should have called her more often. I should have shared the full Gospel message sooner. Would it have made any difference? Probably not, but here's the rub—I'll never know because now, it was too late. It was too late for Sheila.

Thankfully, since the early 1980s, effective treatments—cognitive behavioral therapy, well-tolerated medications, and trans-cranial magnetic stimulation—have increased our tools for treating this debilitating illness. In any given year, 6.7 percent of Americans will suffer with major depression, and over 35,000 will kill themselves. Suicide remains the seventh leading cause of death in American men, despite the newer therapies now available. Even in the days of Hamlet, depression and suicide plagued us, as Shakespeare so eloquently penned below:

"How weary, stale, flat and unprofitable seem to me
all the uses of this world!
'Tis an unweeded garden that grows to seeds.
Things rank and gross in nature possess it merely."

~ **WILLIAM SHAKESPEARE**

The Bizarre Rash that Left Me Scratching My Head

Three exhausting years of internship and residency were finally over. Hallelujah! I had aged ten years in the process, but the grind was worth it. I was now a full-fledged, board-certified internist ready to open my practice.

I designed and decorated my new waiting room with framed and matted Monet and Cezanne prints. Philodendrons and ficus trees, scattered amongst the indigo and burgundy Queen Anne's chairs, added a homey touch. I couldn't help but wander through the office delighted that this day had finally arrived. The young married-couples class from my church hosted a party to celebrate the milestone.

Opening day arrived, and I warmly greeted my first patient. I

escorted her back to an exam room. She yanked up her sweater to display odd splotches across her back and abdomen. "I've got this weird rash, and I don't know what it is."

I stared at her bizarre rash, and panic rippled through me. *That makes two of us!*

I inquired about new detergents, body lotions, foods, medications, or other allergens, but no easy answers emerged. I began to sweat, and I wanted to bolt from the office. I had no clue what was causing her rash; I'd never seen anything like it. My very first patient, and I couldn't diagnose her? This didn't bode well!

What if I was this inept with my next patient? What if I couldn't diagnose a single patient I saw today? What if they all stormed out of my office in disgust and told all their friends I was incompetent? Worse still, what if I misdiagnosed someone, caused them to die, and then got slapped with a hefty malpractice suit?

Panic churned in my stomach like tubes of blood in a centrifuge. Eleven years of education down the drain—and my reputation left in tatters.

I trumped up an excuse to leave the exam room, and I dashed into my office. I shut and locked my door so my new nurse wouldn't see me diving into my dermatology books searching for a picture that looked like this woman's rash. I didn't want her whispering to patients they should seek care elsewhere because the new doc was clueless.

I frantically thumbed through two dermatology books with no luck. Sweat poured down my face as I yanked out a third. Thank the Lord! I found a picture of the rash: Pityriasis rosea. I skimmed the page for everything I could learn and then re-entered my patient's exam room.

With an authoritative tone I said, "Mindy, you have a rash called Pityriasis rosea, felt to be caused by a virus. Its distinguishing feature is a large herald patch, usually on the back.

Pityriasis rosea comes from the Latin word . . . and it lasts from three to eight weeks . . . it is not particularly contagious . . . blah, blah, blah."

From my confident dissertation, she would never guess that five minutes earlier, I was one step from a full-blown anxiety attack.

This wouldn't be the last time in my twenty-plus years of medical practice that I would be stumped, but it was definitely my most nerve-racking. I have since learned saying, "I don't know, but I'll research it until I do," is okay.

"My salad days, when I was green in judgment."

~ **WILLIAM SHAKESPEARE**

How $\mathcal{NOT}$ to Collect a Urine Sample

I wiped my brow in relief as the first patient exited the office believing I was an expert in all things dermatologic. I only hoped my next patient would pose less of a challenge.

Fat chance of that!

Just one glance at Gertrude Stanley, and I knew she had Alzheimer's or some kind of dementing neurological condition. Her torn and improperly snapped bathrobe covered with breakfast jam and oatmeal, her hair sticking out like Bozo the Clown, and her vacuous eyes all hinted her best days had come and gone. Her daughter Betty, a woman sturdy enough to qualify as an offensive lineman for the Green Bay Packers, accompanied her.

After completing the history and physical, I sent Gertrude to the bathroom to obtain a urine sample. After ten minutes, her daughter went to check on her.

Suddenly, I heard Betty shouting and cursing at her mother at decibels loud enough to deafen patients in the office next door. Gertrude had not only provided a sample of urine but also of feces—and unfortunately, not just a sample! Gertrude had scooped runny poop out of the toilet with her bare hands and had tried to cram it into the small urine specimen container. She had then dropped the container on the floor, spattering the revolting mess everywhere.

Her daughter, horrified at the sight, screamed at her mother, "What the &#$@ did you do? Look at you—you're covered in s***. S*** on your hands, s*** on your bathrobe, s*** on your slippers, all over the floor, all over the sink. You even got it on the doorknob and faucet handles. Somebody could slip and crack their head open. Is that what you want?"

Gertrude muttered a shamefaced apology to Betty then tried to hand me the stool-covered specimen container. "Here's the urine you asked for."

I snatched several paper towels and took the nasty cup from Gertrude. Meanwhile, according to my receptionist, Betty had screamed at her mother so loudly, the entire waiting room froze, turned green, and stiffened in their chairs. Who would want to use the patient bathroom now?

Betty lit back into her mother: "What were you thinking? You got nothing but %&$# for a brain, you stupid old lady."

I had heard enough! Yes, Gertrude had created a sickening stench and health hazard, but she was demented, and she couldn't help herself. She didn't deserve public humiliation or such flagrant disrespect from her own daughter.

After washing her up, I escorted Gertrude and Betty out of the office. I then tackled the repulsive chore of cleaning and sterilizing the patient bathroom since my new medical assistant conveniently informed me her job description didn't include cleaning up feces, and she would probably vomit if I made her do it. Well, cleaning poop off the floor wasn't in my job description either, I sputtered to myself as I scrubbed. Eleven years of higher education for this?

Since all my patients had conveniently bee-lined out of the office to avoid

"Let's get a urine sample."

the bathroom bedlam, I tackled the unpleasant task by holding my breath and wearing rubber gloves. I developed a new respect for the poor certified nurse technicians who got stuck doing thankless chores like this on a daily basis.

Surprisingly, Gertrude turned into an interesting case. She didn't have Alzheimer's disease after all. When her daughter mentioned increasing imbalance, urine incontinence, and progressive memory loss, I immediately thought of a rare neurological condition called normal pressure hydrocephalus. When further testing confirmed the diagnosis, a neurosurgeon placed a shunt from her brain into her abdominal cavity to drain the excessive fluid in her brain. Her symptoms improved dramatically.

Unfortunately, her daughter's verbal abuse did not. I ended up reporting Betty for elder abuse. With counseling and strict oversight, Betty's behavior improved, though I sure hope my kids treat me with more dignity when I get old!

"God, grant me the senility to forget
the people I never liked,
the good fortune to run into the ones I did like,
and the eyesight to tell the difference."

~ AUTHOR UNKNOWN

Pick a Day, Any Day

Perhaps news of the bathroom misadventure spread because after my first week, I wasn't seeing any patients. I couldn't understand why. The office phone rang regularly, and I could hear my new receptionist talking to potential patients. However, they wouldn't schedule an appointment. What was up with that? I freaked out when I only had six patients at the end of two weeks. Why wasn't my practice growing?

Not until I overheard the following phone conversation between my receptionist and a potential patient did I figure it out.

> **Patient:** *"I'd like to schedule an appointment with Dr. Burbank."*
> **Receptionist:** *"When would you like to come in?"*
> **Patient:** *"What days and times are available?"*
> **Receptionist:** *"Oh, pick a day, pick a time. Any day, any time."*

A long pause . . . Then, the worried patient inquired, "Doesn't she have any other patients?"

"Not really—six, seven max." She cradled the phone with her neck so she could continue buffing her nails.

The horrified patient said, "Six patients? *That's all?*" She whispered into the phone, "Is something *wrong* with this doctor? I mean, she is *competent*, isn't she?"

Instead of explaining I had only opened my practice two weeks ago but was otherwise an excellent internist and could devote extra time to the patient's every symptom and concern, my receptionist snapped, "How should I know if she's competent? She isn't *my* doctor—I just work here."

Slam! The patient hung up without scheduling an appointment. No wonder my medical practice wasn't growing!

Since the receptionist seemed more eager to manicure her nails than to book my patients, I fired her; now she could spend *all* day filing her nails.

> *"I don't want yes-men around me. I want everyone to tell the truth, even if it costs them their jobs."*
>
> ~ SAMUEL GOLDWYN

The A–t of Hiring and Firing Employees

I learned my very first month one of the biggest challenges of running a medical practice is hiring and managing employees. In the last twenty-five years, I have unintentionally hired a methadone addict, an embezzler, multiple dingbats, two dyslexics (not an asset when their job was filing), and a receptionist who insisted she had to clock in at seven each morning to get caught up on work but actually spent the full hour knitting and browsing the Web. She then demanded I pay her time and a half for her overtime.

Luckily, I spotted most lemons from their résumés and never bothered to interview them. Here are examples of statements written by prospective employees in their résumés or cover letters:

"I would make you a grate medikal secretery because I am atentive to detale." (Five misspellings in one sentence, and you're attentive to detail??)

"Even though I have never drawn blood or administered shots, I could learn this on the job." (Wouldn't that be popular with my patients? Here's hoping she picked up phlebotomy faster than I did, or my practice would never grow!)

"While I've only worked in fast food, I've watched *Scrubs* and *ER* for years, so I know a lot about the medical field."

"My last twelve bosses were sorry to see me leave." (And after four months, I'd become number thirteen.)

"I am, hands-down, the most qualified applicant to apply for this job." (She'd read all the other résumés, had she?)

"I am highly skilled at, and comfortable with, computers. I love being online." (Interpretation: she'll spend all day on Facebook.)

"People tell me I'm the friendliest, most outgoing person they have ever met." (Interpretation: she'll spend all day jabbering with co-workers instead of getting her work done.")

"After a one-month stay in the psychiatric ward, I feel able to work again."

"I am independently wealthy and don't need to work. I *choose* to work because I LOVE medical billing." (*Love medical billing?* Do I look stupid? Nobody loves haggling with insurance companies.)

Thankfully, I didn't fall for the last one. Evidently, she was independently wealthy because she had embezzled a half-million dollars over a five-year period from her last employers. She was independently wealthy all right—her wealth was independent of the paycheck she legally earned! No wonder she loved her job!

Another applicant answered her cell phone to talk to her mother in the middle of her interview, and that didn't include her incognito texting.

Three months after I fired one incompetent employee, I got a call from her husband informing me, "Maggie won't be in for work today. She's in the hospital with a suspected stroke." When I informed him *she'd been fired three months ago,* I found out *she'd never told her husband* and had even gone to great lengths to deceive him. Each morning, she'd dressed professionally, given her husband a quick kiss on the cheek, and supposedly driven to my office. She even called him over the lunch hour to talk about how her day was going! Unfortunately, her incompetence (the reason I'd fired her) was due to an OxyContin addiction, and the "stroke" that caused her slurred speech and stumbling gait was really just an overdose of OxyContin.

How could I forget the morbidly obese applicant who showed up for her interview in see-through white pants and a black thong?

One medical assistant seemed to think all my patients with strep throat were sopranos for the Nashville Opera Company. When they came in sick, she'd mark in the medical record that the patient had a "soar" throat.

I so appreciate my current staff, a competent and loyal group who has worked with me for years. After the deadbeats I've interviewed and hired over the years, they are gems, every one of them!

"I always give 100 percent at work:
10 percent Monday, 23 percent Tuesday,
40 percent Wednesday, 22 percent Thursday,
and 5 percent Friday!"

~ **AUTHOR UNKNOWN**

Your First Appointment is When???

I wasn't the only doctor in town to hire a dingbat. Three years ago, I fractured my foot by stepping into a mole hole in our front yard. Since I had already obtained the X-ray and confirmed the fracture, I called the office of my favorite foot orthopedic and informed his receptionist about my dire need for a plastic healing boot.

Imagine my disgust when she responded, "Let's see, Dr. Bone's first opening is in two months. Can you come in October 13 at 9:30 a.m.?"

A two-month wait for a fractured foot? Wonder how long she'd make me wait for a sprain—a year?

"DR. BONE'S FIRST OPENING FOR A NEW PATIENT IS 2 MONTHS FROM NOW. WILL THAT WORK FOR YOU?"

When I pointed out to this neuron-challenged secretary that perhaps I shouldn't walk around on a fractured foot for two whole months before consulting with the orthopedic, she scrolled down her computer screen then said, "Okay, since you refer a lot of patients to Dr. Bone, I'll fit you in on September 12 at ten. Will that work?"

Gee, thanks! Now I'd only have to limp around on my fractured foot a month!

Where did Dr. Bone find this gem—Pluto?

I asked for her name and scribbled it down so I would never hire her myself; once Dr. Bone figured out what a dingbat he'd hired, she'd be looking for a new job. I then told her I'd try calling a different orthopedic.

Interestingly, Dr. Payne had a no-nonsense receptionist who made Iceland seem balmy, but at least she had the brains to schedule me with the physician's assistant that very afternoon so I could obtain an appropriate healing boot.

"If her brains were dynamite,
there wouldn't be enough to blow off her hat."

~ KURT VONNEGUT

Early Years
in Practice

My Name Was Joe

Thanks to my friendly, competent new receptionist, Andrea, I was now booking patients again, albeit at times, rather strange ones. But doctors with a truckload of medical school loans can't be too choosy. Take Joanna, for example:

Trashy and cheap—the words flashed through my mind the minute Joanna, a lanky woman with over-teased platinum-blond hair, enough eye shadow to paint a barn, and skin-tight jeans, ambled her way into my exam room. Her huge breasts, heaving through a tight, low-cut top screamed, "Boob job," like a Las Vegas neon sign. Her voice, smoky and low, rasped with a tone some men find sexy, but to me, it hollered heavy smoker and lung-cancer risk.

I mentally spanked myself with my stethoscope for harboring such unflattering thoughts toward a patient. Even if she was a trollop, Joanna deserved a compassionate and tolerant doctor. I stretched out my hand, and with a friendly smile, introduced myself. She extended a boxy hand sporting two-inch red nails.

After inquiring about her symptoms, family history, and allergies, I rattled off my usual new-patient questions: "Have you had any surgeries before?"

"Yes," she mumbled in her gravelly voice. "I had my sex organs removed."

"Oh, a hysterectomy," I said, glancing up.

"Um, not exactly." She averted her eyes.

"Your ovaries?" I offered.

"Not them."

"Fallopian tubes? Vagina?" I threw out helpfully.

"No, not them either," she said, squirming in her chair.

I pursed my lips in thought. Okay, she had me stumped. *What other female sex organs were there?*

She must have read my perplexed expression because she mumbled, "I had a sex change operation. My previous name was Joe."

Bedside Manner 101: never reveal to a patient she has totally shocked you. Stay calm and act nonchalant—like every female patient you doctor used to be a man.

"I see," I responded without missing a beat. "So when and where was your surgery?"

"Zurich 1988."

I scribbled frantically in her chart, trying not to show she'd rattled my cage so hard the canary had fallen off its perch, and my brain was now a pile of birdseeds.

The sex change operation *did* explain her unusually narrow hips, six-foot stature, deep voice, boxy hands, and need for breast augmentation surgery!

Now came the real dilemma: do I offer her a Pap smear? The woman had no real female organs so it wasn't necessary, but isn't enduring a Pap smear one of the rites of passage that ushers a girl into womanhood? If I didn't offer it, would she feel slighted? Like I didn't really accept her as a woman? Or worse yet, discriminated against? Would some hungry lawyer take up her cause and sue me for discrimination against transsexuals because I hadn't treated her like every other woman?

On the other hand, if I did offer a Pap smear, would she laugh in my face and snap, "Why would I need that? I don't have any female organs?" Or if I offered a mammogram, would she grab her fake breasts and shove them toward me saying, "Hello! These are just silicon!" I'd look like a fool, like someone who had failed Human Anatomy class. We both know I didn't fail that as I scored in the top *eleven* percentile, remember?

In the end, I decided to be honest and explain why I didn't feel a Pap smear or mammogram was necessary. She agreed with me, and thankfully, no bloodthirsty lawyer came prowling.

Celebrities like Chaz Bono have enlightened us all to the struggles of transsexuals. I would not even bat an eye if Joanna came into my office today. In 1989, however, the medical community often viewed gender-conflicted individuals as freaks. I have doctored two others since Joanna; both were pleasant and surprisingly normal.

"Bisexuality immediately doubles your chances for a date on Saturday night."

~ Rodney Dangerfield

The *Real Reason* Mrs. Talbot Chose Me as Her Doctor

I loved my next patient, Mrs. Talbot, a feisty ninety-eight year old who still walked a mile each day and took no medications. I inquired how she had heard about me and why she had chosen me as her doctor. Had word of my brilliance and stellar bedside manner spread already?

She smirked. "My last three doctors all kicked the bucket. I figured if I picked a real young one fresh out of school, I might stand a sporting chance of dying before my doctor this time."

So much for brilliance and stellar bedside manner.

"I'm not sure I want you as a patient," I retorted with a grin on my face. "Your track record with physicians leaves a lot to be desired. I need to at least get my medical-school loans paid before I kick the bucket."

She waved a dismissive hand at me. "Don't worry. At ninety-eight, I'm bound to drop dead any day now. I've been living on borrowed time for decades."

Every year, like clockwork, she breezed in for her annual physical as perky as ever, her mind keen, her wit intact, and her gait limber. At age 105, she died, the oldest patient I'd ever doctored. While I'll miss Mrs. Talbot's spunk, I was secretly relieved her curse of outliving her doctors had ended!

"You know you're old when the candles cost more than the cake."

~ BOB HOPE

Seaweed Wraps

Chomping hard on the inside of my cheeks to keep from laughing has proven a useful skill over the years, especially the day Louise Thomas came in for an office visit. After escorting her to the exam room, I offered up the usual pleasantries. "Hello, Mrs. Thomas. How are you today?"

She grinned. "I just finished a seaweed wrap, so I feel great."

"A seaweed wrap?" I asked, cocking a brow. Give me canned soup any day!

Sensing my skepticism she waved a hand at me. "They're simply marvelous. You really should try one."

"What restaurant serves seaweed wraps?" I asked, being polite. (Plus, I'd make a mental note never to eat there.)

She laughed. "It's not something you *eat*, silly. It's a spa treatment. They wrap you from the neck down in seaweed, and then you sit in the steam room for an hour so your pores can absorb all the wonderful nutrition of the seaweed."

This was when my cheek-chomping skill came in handy. The mental picture of eighty-year-old Mrs. Thomas wrapped like a mummy from the neck down in green

"It's made from seaweed, bee pollen, fish oil and organic dirt, but the magazine says it tastes exactly like chocolate cake!"

slime tickled my unwrapped funny bone. I envisioned asking the spa employee what she did for a living. "Oh, I wrap ladies in seaweed all day." Now *there's* a career path I'd never considered.

I managed to contain myself enough to ask, "How much do they charge for a seaweed treatment?"

"One hundred fifty dollars," she said without missing a beat.

She then insisted I write an order for these "medically necessary treatments" on my prescription pad so she could write them off on her taxes as a medical treatment. "It's a wonderful source of iodine," she enthused. She could buy a *truckload* of iodized Morton's salt for that price!

I told her I'd have to investigate if seaweed wraps were deemed a legitimate medical tax deduction before I wrote the prescription. I also made a mental note to investigate the price of seaweed. How was it this seaweed spa made more money dumping a woman in a steam room wrapped in seaweed for an hour than I eked out of Medicare by performing and documenting a comprehensive history and physical exam on a deaf, older person with a zillion complaints?

I was clearly in the wrong business! Maybe my time would be better spent scavenging the beaches of Panama City for seaweed. Or maybe I should install a steam room in my office. Patients could get their blood drawn, their EKG, their annual physical, *and* their . . . seaweed wrap?

"Sure, there's plenty of fish in the sea, but there's also sharks, seaweed, crabs, piranhas & toxic waste."

~ **AUTHOR UNKNOWN**

Coffins: Not Just for Corpses Anymore!

Peter Long and his wife were two of my favorite patients—brilliant, funny, and kind. In fact, they became friends as much as patients.

At age seventy-four, Pete was in good health until the day he was rushed to the ER after his wife suspected he was having a stroke. When I asked what alerted her to a problem, she laughed and provided this explanation:

They were at a funeral parlor attending the calling hours of a well-loved neighbor. The new widow was trying her best to provide iced tea for all the visitors, as it was a humid summer day. The small container of ice kept running out, however, necessitating trips back and forth to the kitchen for more ice.

After her *third* trip to the kitchen for ice, Pete pointed to the coffin and offered, "You know, if you'd just get rid of that dead

"I'm sorry, but the comfort of our coffins has never been an issue before!"

SALLY WILLARD BURBANK, MD

body in there, you could sure store a lot more ice in that big box. It would save you trips to the kitchen."

The new widow and my patient's wife stared at him aghast. *Did he really say that? Was he trying to be funny?*

Pete's wife rushed him straight to the emergency room; she knew her husband would *never* have uttered such a tasteless and insensitive remark in his right mind. Turns out, she was right! The MRI revealed a new stroke in the part of his brain that controls impulsivity and reasoning.

Needless to say, I was impressed with Mrs. Long's intuition to suspect a stroke as the cause of her husband's tacky remark.

"There's one thing in this world which isn't ever cheap.
That's a coffin.
Undertaking?
It's the dead-surest business in Christendom!"

~ MARK TWAIN

I Vote for Barney!

Speaking of tacky, it didn't take long for Anita Graves to figure out that her mammography technician could win the the blue ribbon for unprofessional conduct. I learned of the deadbeat employee at Anita's annual physical. She sputtered, "So help me, I've a good mind to sue that woman or have her arrested for assault and battery." She crossed her arms over her breasts, as though trying to protect them from further abuse.

What on earth happened? While all women fuss and whine about their yearly mammogram, none had ever threatened to sue before! Sure, one patient equated her mammogram to a cement truck squeezing her from a 38DD to a 32AA, and another claimed she now knew what being run over by a Mack truck felt like, but Anita wasn't the whiny type. I asked her to explain what happened.

Apparently, the technician crammed Anita's ample breast behind the metal mammogram plate that squeezes the breast, then she cranked up the pressure until her breast was thinner than a crepe. She was about to snap the X-ray when her cell phone rang. Instead of ignoring her personal phone call and completing the mammogram, the technician abandoned her patient with a hasty "Excuse me for a second," and bolted to the adjoining room to answer her phone! Meanwhile, poor Anita Graves stood topless, arm contorted in an awkward position, and breast strangled by the merciless mashing mammogram machine. Imagine her

Yes I did have a Mammogram Today ... Why do you Ask?

John Wise

disgust when she overheard the following phone conversation from the next room:

"Matt, I *know* Josh likes Thomas the Tank Engine, but he loves Barney, too, and Barney would look so adorable on his cake."

The husband must have thought Barney was too girlish because the technician said, "Oh, come on! Barney is not sissy for a three year old."

Anita grit her teeth. *That girl left me stranded in this torture device to discuss a kid's birthday party?*

The technician droned on. "We can always do Thomas the Tank Engine next year, and I saw the cutest little Barney cups and plates and . . . "

Unable to stand the pain another second, Anita hollered into the adjoining room, "I vote for Barney! Now get in here, and get me out of this thing!"

Turns out, the technician *thought* she had loosened the X-ray plates *before* she answered her personal phone call. Profoundly embarrassed, she apologized for her mistake, but with a swollen, bruised breast, Mrs. Graves was in no mood for excuses. After they completed the films, Anita stormed out swearing she would never come back. I can't say I blamed her!

My stomach dropped to the floor when two days later Anita's mammogram report came back stating she needed *additional views* to glean a more accurate picture of a questionable area in her left breast. I dreaded the phone call so much I did what any physician would do—I punted the undesirable chore to my nurse!

"Big or little, you are wonderful just the way you are."

~ **BARNEY**

A *New Way* to Obtain a Breast Reduction?

Doris Lamar had a bust line that made Dolly Parton look flat. Her well-endowed 40GGG-sized chest only caused her back pain and unattractive bra-strap indentations in her shoulder blades, however. Finding clothes that fit properly proved next to impossible. She desperately wanted a smaller bust line, so I completed the appropriate paperwork to obtain insurance approval for breast-reduction surgery. Unfortunately, the insurance company claimed her particular policy did not cover this type of surgery. Ever. For any reason.

Doris would not be deterred, though. She had breast reduction surgery so ingrained in her mind, she was determined to reduce her breast size one way or another. Thus, at her annual mammogram, she told the technician, "Crank that thing down so hard my breasts are mashed flat as a pancake. Maybe that will make the girls smaller." The technician laughed but informed her breast reduction is NOT an FDA-approved indication for mammography!

"They tell me I have pretty feet and I'd like to see them."

www.CartoonStock.com

Marriage,
Motherhood
& Medicine

Before the Baby Comes

Tonya was the first friend I made after moving from Vermont to Nashville. Since we were both in the medical field, and both enjoyed walking, gardening, and laughing, she quickly became a dear friend. Besides attending a weekly church group together, we hoofed it around the Vanderbilt track on a regular basis in our mutually unsuccessful attempts to lose weight.

Tonya had always wanted to be a mother, but for five frustrating years, she had never conceived, despite Pergonal shots and surgery for endometriosis. We all rejoiced when she finally conceived, but then at three months, the unthinkable happened. She miscarried. I cried with her at the loss of her baby and her hope.

The painful saga continued for six more years. Every month started hopeful but ended with bitter disappointment. Since I knew she and her husband would make ideal parents, I prayed regularly, but no further pregnancies occurred.

Unlike Tonya, I was ambivalent about motherhood. Did I really want to lose all my free time, money, and sleep? Did I want to deal with nasty diapers and whining? What if I turned into a cranky, inept mother? What if my children turned into selfish brats, drug addicts, or lazy bums? In short, I was afraid to rock the boat, or in this case, the cradle.

My husband wanted children, however, and I knew he'd make a fantastic father. When I turned thirty-one, he tossed out the gentle hint, "You're not getting any younger, dear." As a doctor, I already knew birth defect rates increased after age thirty-five, and with Tonya's experience that conceiving might take years, I decided to let nature take its course. "We're not going to try," I insisted. "We're just not going to prevent it. If it's meant to happen, it'll happen." I figured with our hectic schedules, it would take months, maybe even years, so I had plenty of time, right?

WRONG! Try one month. I couldn't believe it! The very first month we stopped birth control, I conceive? My husband bounced around the room like Tigger, while I retched into the toilet, nauseated and in shock.

Once I was over morning sickness, I warmed up to the idea of motherhood, except for the overwhelming guilt that consumed me every time I walked the track with Tonya. Why me and not her? She had yearned for a baby for years and had tried so hard. Me? I get pregnant the first month without trying. It wasn't fair.

I dreaded telling her, and for months, I didn't. Instead, I begged God to bless her with a pregnancy before I had to tell her. By my sixth month I began to show, and I couldn't delay any longer. When I told her, she cried. "I didn't know you even wanted a baby." Talk about guilt. I felt like roadkill that deserved to be eaten by turkey vultures.

I petitioned God even more on her behalf. I researched promising scripture verses and Old Testament stories of infertile women who eventually conceived: Sarah, Rebekah, Rachel, and Leah. As I prayed, I begged God to bless Tonya, just as He had these biblical matriarchs. I also added a caveat: *please make it happen before my baby is born.* I knew it would rub acid on her pain to watch me cuddle my newborn son when she remained barren. The last thing I wanted was for my blessing to hinder our friendship. Day and night I uttered the same prayer: "Please, God, bless Tonya with a baby and let her conceive before my baby is born."

Eight months into my pregnancy, my water broke, and nine hours later, at 8:00 a.m. on October 4, my wonderful son, Steven, made his grand debut. Instant love and joy flowed through me as I gazed into the eyes of my sweet blessing from God.

Once Steven was asleep, Nathan and I called our friends and

family with the news. I dreaded calling Tonya. I was so disappointed with God. Never had I prayed with as much faith, consistency, and fervor as I had prayed for Tonya. Alas, I had nothing to show for it. Nada.

Well, I might as well get it over with.

When I made the dreaded call, she sounded surprisingly upbeat and promised to come by later that day for a visit.

After "oohing and ahhing" and agreeing that yes, Steven *was* the cutest baby on the planet, Tonya said, "I'm dying to tell you something. I found out at seven this morning I'm pregnant!"

My mouth dropped. *She was pregnant?* Tears welled up in my eyes, and I couldn't stop grinning. God had not only answered my prayer—He'd timed it to the very *hour*!

I knew I wasn't the only one who had prayed for Tonya, of course. Her husband, family, friends, prayer group, and even a missionary in Japan were all lifting her up in daily prayer. Many had even fasted, but God's timing—*to the very hour*—was God's special blessing to *me*; it was God's reminder that He listens to the prayers of those who pray without ceasing *if* the prayers are in line with His purposes.

Nine months later, Tonya delivered a healthy, beautiful baby girl. Both our children are in their twenties now. Her daughter filled the painful void in her life and has grown into a beautiful woman of God.

I may not always understand God's ways or His timing, but this experience confirmed I could trust God. If I pray with consistency and faith, He does answer prayer.

"The prayer of the righteous is powerful and effective."

~ JAMES 5:16 (NIV)

How Bad Is *Your* Pain?

We had everything worked out, my medical partner and I. She would fly off and lounge on the beach for a week while I held down the fort at the office. She would then return rejuvenated and ready to cover my one-month maternity leave. Since my due date wasn't until November 4 and she'd be back by October 10, we felt certain all would go as planned.

Only problem? We'd neglected to obtain baby Steven's input.

No sooner had my partner boarded the plane and buckled up her seatbelt when my water broke, and I doubled over with contractions. Every four minutes, a knife stabbed my innards and twisted until I threatened to sue Dr. Lamaze for his ridiculous claim that breathing exercises could rid me of this pain. Try a wheelbarrow full of morphine.

Just then, my pager went off. I grabbed it off my belt and after perusing the phone number, I groaned. *Wanda.* One of the few patients who paged me so often I'd programmed her number into my cell phone's speed dial. A pleasant but neurotic hypochondriac, Wanda pestered me regularly with panic attacks she just *knew* were heart attacks. Never mind she'd had a normal cardiac catheterization, echocardiogram, Holter monitor, cardiac event monitor, ultrasound, and a comprehensive GI work-up, all showing nothing. She refused to fill the medications I prescribed for panic disorder or to seek counseling because, despite all the normal tests, she was *still* convinced her heart was diseased!

When my latest contraction died down, I called Wanda. "This is it," she insisted. "The big kahuna. The heart attack that will do me in for sure." I listened patiently as she droned on and on. Heart palpitations and shortness of breath, tingling all over and feelings of doom . . . the exact same symptoms she'd called about last week and the week before that and the week before that.

Even a cat only has nine lives!

Just then, a contraction hammered me so intensely I could only keep from screaming by mentally cursing Eve for eating that stupid apple. This was all her fault—and Nathan's. I grabbed the edge of the bed and held my breath as Wanda continued her monolog: "My hands shake, my breath is short, I'm weak, my heart is pounding, my chest hurts, and . . . "

Clutching the phone, I flopped onto the floor flat on my back, hoping a change in position would lessen the excruciating pain. No such luck. I clenched my teeth and forced out, "On a scale of one to ten, how bad is your pain, Wanda?" *Mine's a hundred!*

Five minutes later, Wanda's panic attack dissipated, and we ended the call. My pain? Worse than ever. In fact, I could have sworn someone was performing a hysterectomy on me without anesthesia.

Nate rushed me to the hospital, and after a whole night of labor, Steven was born at 8:00 a.m. healthy, adorable, and shrieking. After nursing, however, he fell into a sound sleep.

Now came the sticky problem of my four hospital patients. By hospital guidelines, patients had to be evaluated every twenty-four hours. Since my medical partner was two thousand miles away, that left only me.

Thus, as soon as the obstetrical nurse completed her morning assessment on me and left the room, I flung off my hospital gown and dove into my doctor scrubs. Just as I was about to sneak out of the room, my husband said, "Shouldn't you let the nurse know where you're going?"

"Don't be an idiot," I snapped. A ten-hour workday, no sleep, eight hours of hard labor, and plummeting hormones had done little to sweeten my disposition. "They would absolutely forbid me leaving the room to round on patients an hour after childbirth. Women can pass out, hemorrhage, fall into epileptic fits, go psychotic, and start talking to their IV poles. No nurse in her right mind would allow me to leave."

"Then should you be doing this?" he inquired, concern etched across his brow.

"Of course not!" I bolted from the room and charged toward the first patient's room before he could stop me.

Talk about depressing. Not a single patient even *noticed* I'd given birth since yesterday's visit! One patient even had the audacity to ask, "When's that baby due?" Since she was high-risk for a haircut—let alone shocking news—I responded vaguely, "Oh, you know babies. They have a timetable all their own—no matter how inconvenient for the mother." (If she only knew!)

Once I'd completed morning rounds (without seizure, syncope, or psychotic break, I might add), I slithered back to my hospital room, changed back into my patient gown, and crawled into bed—the ideal patient. What the nurses didn't know . . .

That weekend was the first of many challenges in my attempt to combine medicine with motherhood, but my two wonderful children have made it all worthwhile.

"Death, taxes and childbirth! There's never any convenient time for any of them."
~ MARGARET MITCHELL

My Office: The Medical *Milking* Parlor

As a child, my family doctor was an elegant man attired in a tailored shirt, classy tie, and crisp lab coat. Every hair in place, every word a cornucopia of wisdom, his presence was the epitome of confidence and grace. His was a tough act to follow, and even more so after the birth of my first child.

Brainwashed during my pediatrics rotation to believe breast milk was the superior nutritional choice for my newborn son, I was adamant I *would* provide breast milk until he was at least a year old, a choice made possible by my handy double-cupped, electric breast pump. Lofty goals were these, but difficult to do on those hectic clinic days when every patient I saw yanked out a long list of symptoms to discuss and solve.

On one particular day, I was nearly an hour behind schedule, but my breasts—as engorged as cow udders—were right on time. In fact, they had even begun to leak. Soon, my bra and blouse were soaking wet. Thank God for lab coats! I knew I could not delay pumping my breasts any longer, unless I wanted to win a wet T-shirt competition.

I told my medical assistant to obtain a

Even when practiced discreetly, raised eyebrows and disapproving glances still meet with those who dare to udder-feed in public.

By permission of Leigh Rubin and Creators Syndicate, Inc.

urine sample, EKG, and blood draw on my last morning patient while I dashed into my office and relieved the girls from their misery. I now have great compassion for the common Holstein who nuzzles her way to the front of the line outside the parlor door at milking time!

Since Mr. Johnson was a wizened octogenarian with a slow, shuffling gait, I figured I'd have a good ten minutes to suction out the nutritional gold while my nurse completed her nursing tasks.

I dashed into my office, shut the door behind me, flopped into a chair, and assembled the breast pump. I tugged up my bra and connected my now engorged coconuts into the suction cups and flipped on the power switch. Ah, sweet relief as my misery drip, drip, dripped into the baby bottle.

I had just pulled the suction cups off my now happy breasts when Mr. Johnson suddenly opened my office door and barged in. He'd obviously gotten lost on his way back to his exam room and had wandered into my office instead.

Talk about embarrassing! There I sat, topless and with my breasts flaunted like some floozy in a strip club. I yanked down my top, but not before his eyes were wider than moon pies and bulging with shock.

I don't know which of us was more mortified. I blurted out, "Excuse me! I was pumping." His eyes widened further. I then realized an eighty-year-old man probably had no idea what I meant by "pumping." No doubt he thought it was some new-fangled exercise women performed to increase their bust size. Swell! He muttered a hasty apology, shut my office door, and scurried to his exam room. Unfortunately, since I had not yet completed his physical exam, I now had to walk back into his exam room and face him again. I eyed my breast pump long-ingly. If only it could suck me into oblivion. How do I act like a professional after he'd seen me half-naked?

I tugged on my lab coat and slithered into his exam room as

though nothing unseemly had happened. We avoided eye contact and focused on the importance of maintaining excellent blood-sugar control. We discussed side effects of his new cholesterol medication. I wrote out his refills, all the while avoiding eye contact.

Unable to stand the awkwardness another second, I explained I'd just given birth to a baby, and what he'd witnessed was me pumping breast milk to feed my baby. He looked even more uncomfortable. I then deduced men of his generation did not use words like breasts and pumping milk in mixed company, let alone with their woman doctor.

My advice to women everywhere who want to combine a professional career with motherhood: lock your office door!

"Man is the only animal that blushes. Or needs to."

~ MARK TWAIN

How to Scare Your Kids Away from Med School

I had high hopes my daughter, Eliza, would one day follow me into medical school. As a little girl, she boasted how when she grew up, she wanted to become a doctor, just like her Mommy. That is, until the unfortunate day, at age nine, when she spent a few hours in my office after work because my husband was called out of town unexpectedly.

Bored, she milled around the office inspecting my equipment. I alternated between scribbling patient notes and keeping my daughter entertained. I ran an EKG on her and explained what the tracing said about her heart rhythm. I tested her hearing and vision and measured her height and weight. I thumped on her knees with a reflex hammer, and she giggled when her knee jerked forward. I could tell I had sparked her interest in the medical field.

Then came the fateful moment when she pulled out a Hemoccult card from an exam table drawer, held it up, and asked me what it was. I explained it was a test for colon cancer.

She stared at the card and then at me. "How does it work?"

I opened the flaps on the cardboard test and explained how the card worked. "You smear a little pooh-pooh on this square here, and then you apply drops of this solution onto the back side of the square." I had her drip three drops of the clear liquid onto the square. "If this square turns bright blue, it means the patient is passing blood, and that could be a sign of colon cancer."

Her brow furrowed as she stared down at the card. "But how does the pooh-pooh get onto the little square?"

Never one to lie or sugarcoat, I said, "Mommy sticks her finger up the patient's bottom, and then she smears the pooh-pooh onto the little square."

Her eyes doubled in size. "You stick your finger up people's butts?" Complete horror and disgust blanketed her face. "Eeww!!!"

"I wear a rubber glove," I quickly added.

"EEEWWW!" She charged out of the room muttering she couldn't believe her mother did such a nasty thing.

Never again did she mention becoming a doctor. In fact, she embraced feeding baby monkeys in Africa or working for the State Department negotiating peace in the Middle East. In other words, somewhere as far away from Mom's Hemoccult cards as possible!

Words of advice to fellow physicians who dream of their children entering medical school: Hide your Hemoccult cards!

"Children are a great comfort in your old age—and they help you reach it faster, too!

~ LIONEL KAUFFMAN

What a Way to 𝒟𝓇𝓊𝓂 𝒰𝓅 Business!

Patients ask me all the time if my son is following me into medical school. The answer is a resounding "NO!" Not because he isn't smart or driven enough, and not because of the long hours he witnessed his mother working. The reason is far simpler and humorous.

At age seven, I took Steven on hospital rounds with me so a couple of my patients who always asked about my children could meet him. I also thought this would be a great opportunity to expose Steven to the medical field and maybe spark an interest. This was pre-HIPAA-law days, so I wasn't violating any regulations.

We visited a lung cancer patient, and I showed him the large mass on the patient's chest X-ray. He witnessed firsthand a man gasping for breath and wheezing like a teakettle because of his asthma and emphysema. The last patient had recently completed a leg re-vascularization surgery due to blockages in his leg arteries caused from smoking. Steven stared at the intimidating incision that snaked the entire length of the man's leg. His eyes grew bigger than bedpans, and his face blanched whiter than the bandages with which I redressed the patient's incision.

As we left the patient's room, I decided this was an opportune chance to give my "Don't EVER smoke or this could be you" speech. My son accuses me of lecturing him so many times about the evils of smoking and drugs during his growing up years that his eyes were at risk for permanently locking into a rolled up position!

"Steven, every single one of these patients is in the hospital today because of smoking. Lung cancer, emphysema, and blocked leg arteries are all due to cigarettes. In fact, if these patients had never started smoking, not one of them would be in the hospital today." I crossed my arms and waited for the appropriate response: "Why would anyone smoke, Mom?" or better yet, "I'll never smoke!"

Imagine my shock when instead he said, "Mom, if I was a doctor, I'd tell ALL my patients to smoke!"

My mouth dropped in horror. *Did he not get it? Was he stupid?* "Why would I do that, Steven? Smoking is bad for them."

He grinned up at me. "Maybe so, but what a way to drum up business!"

I stared at my future used car salesman—or Enron executive—and mentally erased Harvard Medical School from his career trajectory. Perhaps he needed fewer lectures on smoking and more on ethics!

"Education without values, as useful as it is, seems rather to make man a more clever devil."

~ C.S. LEWIS

An X-Rated Birthday Party

Over the years, I have purchased Thin Mint Girl Scout cookies, wrapping paper, magazine subscriptions, and vitamins to show my support to patients. I have even attended my share of Pampered Chef and Mary Kay parties. Thus, when a patient informed me she hosted at-home parties in hopes of digging her way out of debt, I said, "My daughter has a birthday coming up. I might be interested in hiring you."

"Really?" she said, beaming. "That would be great, though I warn you, I'm not your usual party hostess, as I don't just do balloons and birthday cake at my parties."

Envisioning magic tricks, face painting, and manicures, I replied, "Great! We've already done Chuck E. Cheese's, roller skating, and a mad-scientist party, so we're ready for something different."

She released a nervous laugh. "This would be different, all right."

Since I was running behind schedule, I scribbled down my e-mail address and insisted she send more info. I then made a hasty exit.

Imagine my shock when I got home that night, opened her E-mail, and found out her parties focused on selling sex toys, lingerie, and erotic paraphernalia! Wouldn't that go over well with the parents of my ten-year-old daughter's friends!

I scrolled down further on her web site, hoping to find a more kid-appropriate party. Instead, I was offered a vast selection of chocolate and caramel panties, heated massage oils, garter belts, vibrators, flavored condoms, and tawdry sex games.

I could just picture handing all the girls a party bag stuffed with condoms, dildos, and strip poker cards. In fairness, my patient had warned me her parties weren't just balloons and cake, but I sure hadn't expected this! Did she seriously think I'd host such a party to ten-year-olds?

I sent a polite response declining her offer claiming Eliza had opted for a sleepover party *instead*.

"Every party has two kinds of people—those who want to go home and those who don't.
The trouble is, they are usually married to each other."

~AUTHOR UNKNOWN

Band-Aids 101

Can you think of anything worse than mandatory meetings? Somehow I'd been conned into co-leading my daughter's prekindergarten Girl Scout troop. Despite the hours of preparation involved, I adored cooking up fun activities and field trips for my daughter and her friends. What I *didn't* enjoy were the mandatory training sessions for troop leaders. Two hours of such tidbits as: "Count the number of girls attending a field trip so you don't leave one behind." DUH! Or how about, "Don't offer activities that require reading if your girls can't read." The woman next to me rolled her eyes and passed over a note saying, "You think?"

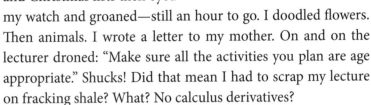

I glanced around to see if others were as bored as we were. All around the room heads bobbed and eyelids drooped. I envied the woman sleeping in the back row, strategically planted behind a large post.

I composed my grocery and Christmas lists then eyed my watch and groaned—still an hour to go. I doodled flowers. Then animals. I wrote a letter to my mother. On and on the lecturer droned: "Make sure all the activities you plan are age appropriate." Shucks! Did that mean I had to scrap my lecture on fracking shale? What? No calculus derivatives?

My favorite tidbit of wisdom: "If you're going on a field trip, make sure all the parents chauffeuring the children know where you're going." The woman next to me rolled her eyes again. My conclusion? Any mother clueless enough to *need* any of this drivel wasn't fit to lead a troop in the first place.

After two hours nine minutes and thirty seconds, they released us from Girl Scout prison. I trudged to my car sputtering; I was half-tempted to send a bill for two wasted hours of my time.

But not wanting to be branded as a troublemaker, I endured each and every training session until I had only one left: First Aid. I snickered. With four years of medical school, three years of residency training, and seven years in private practice, surely they would exempt me from that class!

No such luck.

After leading the troop several years, I received a call from a Girl Scout "Gestapo" admonishing me to complete this final step in my leadership training.

HENRY HEIMLICH AS A
REBELLIOUS *TEENAGER*

"I'm a board-certified internist, and I'm up to date in both Basic and Advanced Cardiac Life Support. I know the Heimlich maneuver. Surely that counts as more medically trained than some two-hour first aid class."

The woman hemmed and hawed. "Nothing in our guidelines states doctors are exempt from the class, so you need to attend."

Are you kidding me??? They require board-certified internists to take a Girl Scouts' first aid class?

I could hardly wait. No doubt this thriller would teach me to apply ice to a sprained ankle, or Neosporin to a cut. They'd tell me not to give medication without clearing it with the parents first. Or the real eye-opener—don't feed peanuts to a girl who's allergic to them.

Desperate for a get-out-of-jail-free card, I asked to speak to the woman's supervisor. I prayed fervently while I explained to the higher up why I felt qualified to medically care for the girls without the Saturday morning first aid lecture.

Yes, I knew to look for ticks after hiking. I carried an EpiPen and children's Benadryl in my car just in case any of the girls developed an unexpected anaphylactic reaction to a bee sting. I kept Neosporin and an ACE bandage in my trunk. I had the phone numbers and allergy list of every girl in my troop.

After my ten-minute dissertation, the supervisor finally agreed I could skip the first-aid class.

Nice to know after fourteen years of medical training and experience, I was now deemed competent in Band-Aids 101.

> *"The door to safety swings on the hinges of common sense."*
>
> ~ AUTHOR UNKNOWN

Isn't Your *Mother* a Doctor?

People often assume the families of doctors get top-notch medical care. After all, they have daily access to a doctor. What more could they want, right? Talk to the spouses of most doctors, though, and you'll find most get subpar care. How can that be, you ask? For starters, doctors are rarely home, and when they are, they're exhausted, cranky, hungry, or burned out on hearing medical complaints all day. Plus, we are not specialists in every field of medicine, though we like to think we are.

Case in point: My daughter has spring allergies, so every March she snivels and drips and rubs her eyes. I'd tried her on several antihistamines, but they either made her sleepy or didn't work at all. Since we only had catastrophic health insurance coverage, allergy shots were cost prohibitive. Eliza hated squirting stuff up her nose, so nasal sprays were out of the question. My conclusion? Spring allergies weren't going to kill her. Besides, they'd be over in a month anyway, right?

My daughter seemed fine with this decision until the day her English teacher, annoyed at her constant sniveling, sneezing, and nose-blowing, snapped, "Eliza, isn't your mother a *doctor*? Why doesn't she *do* something about your allergies?"

Why, indeed.

Another time, my son came home from school upset because another first-grader teased him that his breath smelled like a dead mouse. Incensed, I was ready to call the boy's mother and blast her for raising such a bully—until I got a whiff of his breath, that is. Yuk! His breath *did* smell like a decaying mouse!

Using a butter knife for a tongue depressor, I gagged my son and peered into his throat by shining a flashlight inside his mouth. That's when I noted foul-smelling pus exuding from his tonsil. With a course of penicillin, he and the classmate were soon friends again.

My husband had it the worst. One day he bellyached about a burning pain in his buttock area that radiated down his leg, I was quick to tell him, without even examining him, that he likely had sciatica, caused by lugging his heavy musical equipment in and out of the van. "Give it a few days rest, swallow some ibuprofen, and you'll be better in no time." (A variant of the old "Take two aspirin and call me in the morning" line.)

But two days later, his pain had worsened. The next morning, when he was changing clothes, I happened to notice a crop of blisters on a reddened patch of skin on his buttock.

He doesn't have sciatica—he has full-blown shingles! No wonder he's in pain!

I felt like crawling under the porch. I hadn't performed the careful history and physical examination that I would have for any other patient before pronouncing he had sciatica. What half-baked medical care he received from me. If I'd taken the time to actually examine him, I would have seen the blisters and made the proper diagnosis two days earlier!

If Nathan dares lament about his rotten medical care, however, I reply, "You get what you pay for!"

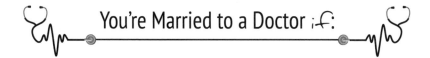

You're Married to a Doctor if:

- Hearing about dismembered body parts or gangrenous bowels during dinner doesn't faze you in the slightest.

- "I'll be home in ten," means ten *hours*, not ten *minutes*.

- Your spouse spends fourteen hours a day around doctors, but hasn't *seen* a doctor in decades.

- People assume *you* know everything medical—by osmosis?

- You embrace ice storms because the patients all cancel their appointments, and your spouse makes it home in time for

CartoonStock.com

"I read your silly email this morning about me not paying enough attention to you..."

dinner for a change. Unless he's a trauma surgeon!

- Patients obtain your home phone number, and you know them all on a first-name basis, along with all their medical problems. As does your twelve year old. And your ten year old.

- Your child takes a knee joint or eyeball for "Show and Tell."

- Your coffee table is piled higher than the Eiffel Tower with medical journals. Your spouse refuses to let you pitch them claiming, "I'm going to read them." Some are three years old. You stealthfully chuck the journals anyway, and she doesn't even notice.

- You sometimes fantasize what life would be like with a spouse with reasonable hours.

- You conclude life would be worse because despite the long hours, weird patient phone calls, piles of medical journals, and sickening dinnertime conversation, you wouldn't want to spend your life with anyone else.

The *Newest* Diagnostic Criterion for Melanoma

Melanoma runs strongly in my husband's family. In fact, two relatives died in their early forties of the dreaded disease, and my father-in-law requires yearly skin checks with a dermatologist. Thus, when I noticed a worrisome new black mole on the back of my husband's upper arm, I was concerned. It displayed all the danger signs for malignancy: size greater than one centimeter, black color, ratty border, and irregular pigment.

I immediately did what I do best in a crisis: borrow trouble.

Mentally, I had him diagnosed with Stage IV malignant melanoma, thus facing a bleak and expensive future with Mohs surgery, chemotherapy, and ultimately, hospice care. He'd be dead by fifty, and I'd be left a lonely widow trying to fund two kids through college all by myself.

I yanked his arm toward me again, hoping I was mistaken. But no, its black color and irregular borders definitely looked worrisome; it needed a biopsy. Not wanting to upset my husband, I pasted on a professional veneer and told him I'd schedule an appointment with a dermatologist as soon as possible.

As luck would have it, the dermatologist had a recent cancellation for that very afternoon. Did I want it? You bet!

Nathan jumped into the shower to clean up before his appointment, and I attempted to quell my panic by deadheading petunias in the flowerboxes.

Others have survived cancer, so can you.

Jesus said, "I will never leave you or forsake you," I reminded myself. Alas, no amount of self-talk or flower pruning removed the worry curdling in my stomach like sour milk.

After Nate climbed out of the shower and dried off with a towel, he hollered out the window to me. "Sally, come quick! Look at this!"

I dashed into the house consumed with fear. *Had he found another irregular mole?*

When I entered the bathroom, however, he was grinning! "Look! It's gone!"

I stared at his upper arm in amazement. *Where had it gone?*

No, it wasn't a miracle from God. Turns out, his "melanoma" was nothing more than dried on Nutella! Nate now remembered eating several spoonfuls of his favorite vice before bed and must have somehow smeared some on his upper arm. When dry, the Nutella mimicked melanoma.

I felt like a fool. Some doctor I was—I couldn't distinguish melanoma from Nutella? Imagine if I'd sent him to the dermatologist to biopsy Nutella! I'd never live it down.

Perhaps the American Dermatological Society should add a new diagnostic criterion for malignant melanoma: doesn't scrub off with soap and water!

"It isn't what we don't know that gives us trouble, it's what we know that ain't so."

~ **WILL ROGERS**

Patients Who
Inspired Me

Until My Dying Breath

Remember the lyrics from a song on TV's *Hee-Haw* that lamented, "If it weren't for bad luck, I'd have no luck at all?" Well, that could have been the theme song of Barbara Brown. Despite enduring enough trials to compose a Grammy-winning country ballad, Barbara was the most inspiring patient I ever doctored.

The seventh of eight children, Barbara was born to an alcoholic mom and a marginally employed, abusive dad. Her mother chugged whiskey at the neighborhood bar most nights and then zonked out on the couch hung over all the next day. Her father, usually drunk, clobbered his wife and kids for the slightest infraction such as burned toast or a minor sibling squabble. In short, Barbara had every excuse to resort to drugs and alcohol—anything to escape the hellhole she was forced to call home. Instead, she found respite at a local church where the pastor's wife and several other ladies ensured she had school clothes, encouragement, and plenty of warm hugs.

To survive the neglect and abuse at home, Barbara's siblings stuck together like a school of guppies. "How could I become bitter when my older sisters worked so hard after school to buy peanut butter, bread, and milk for me? God blessed me with wonderful sisters and a supportive church family, so I had much to be grateful for."

When a handsome classmate, Roger Brown, took an interest in her and proposed marriage after high school, she didn't require much persuading. A road out of Dysfunction Junction—hand me the map and car keys! "When Roger held me in his arms and told me he loved me and would always take care of me, I couldn't believe my luck. I'd always wanted to be a wife and mother, and thanks to Roger, that dream came true."

Over the next twelve years, she bore five active children who kept her running from baseball to football to piano lessons. At forty-two, she delivered a baby girl with Down's syndrome. While many women would feel devastated or overwhelmed with the demands of a mentally challenged child, Barbara adored her baby girl. "You couldn't find a more loving child than my Alice. Her sweet smiles and hugs light up my day."

Life was good until the dreadful day her husband revealed that while he still loved her and didn't want to break up their family, he now realized he was gay and "could no longer deny who I really am."

Barbara was devastated. She had a choice: divorce, or tolerate a husband who caroused at gay bars on Saturday nights. She still loved Roger deeply, and devoutly religious, she didn't believe in divorce, nor did she want to destroy the loving family they had created together. "He's a great father, a good provider, and he doesn't drink or beat me. He's kind and gentle, and we've been through so much together. How can I throw it all away because he has this one issue?"

Tears rolled down her cheeks, and I handed her a tissue, my own eyes pooling. She blew her nose and wiped her eyes with the tissue. "What do I do, Dr. Burbank? He says he still loves me and doesn't want a divorce. I don't want one either." She wrung the tissue between her fingers. "But it kills me every time he leaves on Saturday night. I know exactly where he's going and what he's up to."

Right or wrong, she chose to stay, and she developed a cordial, co-parenting partnership with him. Despite the emotional pain and betrayal, she insisted, "I'm choosing to focus on what's good in Roger, and he has a lot of good qualities."

She channeled her hurt into a quilting group at her church to raise money for an orphanage in Africa. Some of the quilts were so exquisite they fetched over $1,200 apiece. "I might not have a college degree, but I know how to quilt, and God can use any talent we have for His glory."

If a rotten childhood, handicapped child, and gay husband weren't challenging enough, Barbara's health nosedived. First, breast cancer that necessitated a double mastectomy, then chemotherapy, and radiation. Soon, brittle diabetes requiring insulin with every meal and a strict diet controlled her life. A year later, despite daily aspirin and cholesterol-lowering medications, her heart and neck arteries required heart and carotid artery surgery. With time, her vision deteriorated from macular degeneration. Sadly, she could no longer stitch the intricate quilts on which she'd built her reputation.

Did she complain or give up? No! Instead, she started a cooking class for all the newlyweds at her church. "Dr. Burbank, some of these girls can barely boil water! Don't they teach Home Economics anymore?"

Her class was a hit. Some weeks, more than twenty-five women learned to roll a piecrust, baste a roast, and steam vegetables to al dente. The women graced the tables with red plaid tablecloths, cleverly folded napkins, and vases teeming with cheery white daisies. The young wives giggled and glowed as they served home-cooked feasts to a roomful of hungry and grateful husbands.

Unfortunately, Barbara's health declined even further. She suffered such severe lumbar disc disease, osteoarthritis of the knees, and leg swelling that she could only get around in a wheelchair. Worse still, her kidneys failed, requiring thrice-weekly hemodialysis. She was now too weak to cook for herself, let alone teach a class.

To his credit, her husband kept his promise to always take care of her, and he took over the cooking, cleaning, shopping, banking, and nursing care. He drove her to lengthy dialysis treatments every Monday, Wednesday, and Friday, and he carefully divvied out her medicines at the proper time. He prepared a strict diabetic diet and injected her insulin.

Eventually, his strength waned as well, so the couple hired a homemaker to help with the cooking and housekeeping. After several meals of charred burgers and undercooked chicken, they quickly discovered their homemaker couldn't cook! Roger wanted to fire her on the spot. "She's useless," he sputtered. "If I eat any more of her food, I'll land in the hospital with Salmonella!"

Barbara's response? "We can't fire her, Roger. She's a single mother, and she needs this job. If she can't cook, she'll be fired wherever she goes, and then what will happen to her two little girls?"

You guessed it. Barbara, while sitting in her wheelchair, legs propped up to reduce swelling, nearly blind, riddled with arthritis, and requiring thrice-weekly dialysis, taught the "homemaker" how to prepare chicken and dumplings, beef stew, quiche, and meatloaf.

"God put this girl in my life so I could teach her to cook and improve her job skills. I may not be able to walk or read the fine print on recipes anymore, but even in a wheelchair, I can teach her to sift flour and baste a chicken. Until my dying breath, I will bless others any way I can."

Barbara recently passed away, but I will never forget her

make-the-best-of-what-you've-got-left attitude. She looked for ways to bless others with whatever strength and ability she still had left. She found joy, humor, and purpose in life, despite her many setbacks. She chose to recognize the good qualities in a husband, handicapped child, and hired homemaker whom others might condemn or write off as a burden. Abraham Lincoln said it best: "Most folks are as happy as they make up their minds to be."

"A hero is an ordinary person who finds
the strength to persevere and bless others,
in spite of overwhelming obstacles."

~ CHRISTOPHER REEVES

The *Onion* Room

I would have quit that day if I weren't the boss. It started when my first patient arrived thirty minutes late but demanded she still be seen anyway. "It wasn't my fault; traffic was terrible," she insisted. Fine, I'll see you, but now I'm already forty minutes behind schedule, and before long, another patient will shriek at my receptionist about her long wait.

Instead, the next patient screamed at my receptionist for trying to collect her co-pay. After smoothing her ruffled feathers, I entered the next exam room only to be weighed down with a massive pile of forms needing completion by tomorrow. Stir in the twenty minutes on hold with an insurance company, a patient now hostile about the forty-minute wait, and a man who fainted when his blood was drawn, and my day became as enjoyable as a balloon ride in a tornado.

The final straw? Mrs. Smith informed me she had stopped her blood pressure medication a month earlier and had replaced it with an herbal remedy she'd learned about online. The website claimed this 100 percent all-natural herb had "miraculous powers" to lower blood pressure. The miracle is that anyone falls for such boastful, unproven claims.

"I'm just more comfortable going the organic route," she said. "Besides, according to the Internet, the blood pressure pills you prescribed are synthetic poison." She glared at me as though I'd prescribed cyanide.

By stopping her "synthetic poison," her blood pressure now registered a dangerous 220/110. In short, her all-natural, organic herb was nothing more than an expensive placebo. She may as well have swallowed a fistful of crabgrass, but try telling her that! She stormed out of the office in a huff.

I exited her room now a full hour behind schedule. My head pounded like a kettledrum, and my neck muscles felt tighter than a violin string. Could I rip down my medical shingle and join the symphony instead?

I rolled my neck in slow circles and tried to relax my jaw as I inhaled several slow, deep, cleansing breaths. Ah, much better, but not for long. I walked into my office only to face the Leaning Tower of Pisa; my desk was piled so high with charts all needing my attention, I couldn't see over the top of it. I flopped into my chair for a two-minute respite while I tackled the stack of medication refill requests.

What had possessed me to become a doctor? My images of Marcus Welby, MD shared little in common with the modern internist's life—insurance hassles, HIPAA forms, more paperwork, and patients who believed the Internet and Dr. Oz over me.

I scribbled my signature on the last prescription refill request and lugged the unwieldy heap to my medical assistant's desk. The way this day was going, I braced myself for the next disaster. What would it be? A malpractice lawsuit? Power outage? Employee catfight? Today, they all seemed possible.

I bustled into the exam room of my next patient and greeted Sue Moreland, a pleasant forty-year old, who gazed up at me with red, puffy eyes. She looked as though she'd been crying for a month. Had her mother died, or her husband filed for divorce?

Not surprisingly, she'd made the appointment to investigate what could be done for her irritated eyes. One by one I eliminated all of the usual culprits: crying jags due to stress or depression, new eye make-up, pink eye, and allergens. I scratched my head, perplexed. She then offered, "I think it's my job."

I nodded. "I get it—you work in one of those sick buildings we hear about on the news, and now you and your co-workers all walk around with red, swollen eyes."

"No, none of my co-workers are affected. Just me."

I glanced up from writing in her chart. "Why do you think it's your job, then?"

"Cause none of my co-workers are in the onion room."

My eyebrow rose. "The *onion* room?"

The slightest hint of a smile crossed her lips. "I peel and slice onions eight hours a day. That's my job."

I stared at her in disbelief. "You cut up onions *eight hours a day*?" No wonder her eyes were red!

"Yes, and the room is small and unventilated."

Rage welled up in me like a geyser. Surely torturing an employee with an unventilated onion room for eight hours a day must violate OSHA safety laws.

I exited the room, stomped to my office, and rang up the local OSHA officer, ready to demand he investigate and improve her working conditions. Imagine my disgust when he informed me he had already investigated the onion room several times this year, and no laws had been violated. He claimed he couldn't do anything! "Since onions are a natural food and are not a toxin or poison, my hands are tied."

"But her work environment is intolerable. How would you like to chop onions all day?"

"I'd hate it, trust me! The odor is so overwhelming I can hardly stand to walk into the room, let alone inspect it. The turnover for that job is unreal, but unfortunately, since no laws have been broken, my hands are tied."

I returned to Susan's exam room still shaking my head. "How long have you been stuck in the onion room?" I asked.

"Three months. My boss says I've lasted longer than any previous employee," she boasted.

I crossed my arms. "Why on earth do you stay?"

"I hope to be promoted to cabbages," she said, a hopeful lilt in her tone.

"Cabbages?" I bit the inside of my cheeks to keep from laughing.

"Yes—the slaw room. It's the next step up in the company, and it comes with a fifty-cents-an-hour raise. My boss says he'll promote me as soon as he has an opening."

I stared at her in awe, chagrined at my own bad attitude and petty complaints. Here I'd sputtered all morning about a few minor insurance hassles, an overzealous Internet reader, and a heap of paperwork, while this poor woman endured the noxious odor and irritation of onions for eight hours a day—for minimum wage, no less! Yet she not only endured, she remained positive, dreaming about her promotion to cabbages!

Now, whenever I'm having "one of those days," I remind myself things could be worse—much worse. I could be chopping onions.

"Instead of complaining that the rosebush is full of thorns, be happy the thorn bush has roses."

~ CHINESE PROVERB

No More *"Fatty Patty"*

The only thing most women crave more than motherhood is a slim, sexy physique. Patty was no exception, but obesity had plagued Patty her whole life. In grade school, kids taunted, "Fatty Patty." At age fifty, she tipped the scales at 362 pounds. She huffed and puffed with every step, and her knees groaned in agony carrying the massive weight. She required ten medications and insulin to control her diabetes, blood pressure, heartburn, arthritis, and cholesterol.

Like most obese patients, she had tried all the usual diets, but her weight yo-yoed. She was ashamed to be seen in a swimsuit and hadn't flown in decades.

Thus, when Blue-Cross Blue-Shield approved her gastric bypass surgery, she dove in headfirst. By the end of nine months, she had lost one hundred pounds. By two years, she weighed less than one hundred fifty.

When she came in for her office visit, I made her spin around. "Look at you! Your clothes are falling off you!"

She grinned. "They are—literally." She then recounted an embarrassing tale. To save money, she had delayed buying smaller-sized clothes until her weight loss had stabilized.

One day, while standing in line at Walmart, the large

"Cheer up — at least it makes you look taller!"

safety pin she'd used to take in the waist of her pants popped off. Her pants fell to her ankles. There she stood—for shoppers everywhere to see—in oversized underwear and a tank top, with her pants swimming around her flip-flops.

I suggested that perhaps half-price days at Goodwill might offer a safer alternative to time in jail for indecent exposure.

The trials of losing weight only got worse! She and her husband were invited to a large family reunion in Michigan. Since she hadn't seen any of his relatives in five years, she pulled out all the stops to show off her new physique. A fitted emerald-green pantsuit, Spanx, high heels, manicure, and a flattering new hairstyle completed her look. She posed in the mirror and for the first time in her life felt pretty and ready to face her husband's relatives.

She held her breath as she strutted into the reception hall clutching her husband's arm. What would everyone think?

Unfortunately, instead of the glowing compliments she had envisioned in her daydreams, people stared, whispered, gawked, pointed, and even *glared* at her. Not a single person even came up to say hello, let alone compliment her on her weight loss! Had no one noticed? She'd tried so hard, but no gold star. Bitter tears stung her eyes.

Finally, Uncle Joe moseyed up to her husband and whispered, "George, I didn't know you and Patty had split up. Who's the new woman?"

Her husband roared with laughter. "New woman? I'm not divorced, but Patty's lost so much weight I feel like I am married to a new woman. She looks great, doesn't she?" he said, beaming and gesturing with his hand.

Uncle Joe's eyes bulged as he took a second look. "Patty? Is that you?" He stared at her in disbelief, and then grinned. "Why, I didn't even recognize you!" He hugged her and said, "We all thought George had brought some new mistress instead of you. That's why we were all being so standoffish, cause we all love our Patty, fat or thin." He yelled across the room to his wife, "Hey, Sadie. She ain't no mistress—it's Patty! She done lost a lot of weight."

Bedlam ensued, as women crowded around her clucking and hugging and ooh-ing and ahh-ing. No one had even recognized her? They'd thought she was George's mistress?

Hmmm . . . maybe now that she felt attractive, his femme fatale she would be!

"In the Middle Ages, they had guillotines, stretch racks, whips and chains. Nowadays, we have a much more effective torture device called the bathroom scale."

~ STEPHEN PHILLIPS

An Honors Class for Remedial Dieters

I eyed the name of my next patient on the schedule and groaned. Maggie Nelson. Why did I even bother trying to help her? Talk about a waste of time. I had spent hours over the years counseling, encouraging, guilt tripping, and attempting to motivate the butterball to lose weight. Diabetes, high cholesterol, high blood pressure, worn-out knees—the woman needed to drop a good ninety pounds—but I may as well have instructed a Macy's mannequin for all the results I'd seen. She couldn't afford Weight Watchers; her insurance didn't cover gastric bypass; her knees ached, so she couldn't exercise; eating broccoli made her bloat; and artificial sweeteners gave her a headache. When it came to excuses, Maggie could write a bestseller!

I inhaled a deep breath and forced myself to enter Maggie's exam room—might as well get it over with. I perused her chart and scowled. As expected, not only had she not lost a single ounce, she'd actually gained ten pounds. Next came the lame excuses: she'd had out-of-town company, and how could I expect her to lose weight around her birthday and anniversary? Then she claimed she "ate like a bird." Right! An ostrich, maybe. My favorite excuse? She had

"If I gain 20 pounds, it will give me the motivation I need to stick to my diet!"

to keep freshly baked chocolate chip cookies around the house in case the grandkids paid a visit. When I asked how often the grandkids came, she hemmed and hawed and finally admitted they lived out of state.

We danced the same worn-out waltz, Maggie and I. I'd counsel her to exercise more and cut down on sweets and soda. She'd nod, promise to do better, and waddle out of my office, both of us knowing nothing would change.

Then I read Jennie Ivey's story "The Honors Class" in *Chicken Soup for the Soul: The Power of Positive*, a story about a class of remedial history students whose teacher had been falsely informed the class was filled with academic superstars, the "honors" students. Because of her high expectations and the extra effort she poured into these supposed "gifted" scholars, not only did all the students pass, but the majority earned As and Bs. Wow! Remedial students acing honors history? Unheard of.

A twinge of guilt pricked my conscience. Had I prematurely given up hope for patients like Maggie Nelson? Did the quote about "the soft bigotry of low expectations" apply to me? Truthfully, I'd given up on Maggie years ago, but what if I treated my obese diabetics with the same high expectations and extra effort with which Jennie Ivey treated her remedial history students? What if I treated my failing dieters as though they were "Honors" patients?

You'll just be wasting your time, my inner cynic insisted. But no harm trying, my conscience countered.

First, I researched everything I could find from reputable journals and books about people who had lost at least fifty pounds without surgery and maintained the loss for over a year. I discovered the National Weight Loss Registry, which researched and followed over three thousand people who met these criteria. Then I created a notebook of all the winning advice from these weight loss champions. Weekly group support proved helpful to many successful dieters, so I'd start a weight loss support group where I'd teach the principles of the Weight Loss Registry.

At Maggie's next clinic visit, I told her about the group and encouraged her to join. I offered the class for free so money wouldn't be an excuse. She claimed she didn't want to face rush hour traffic every week. That's when I took her to task. "Maggie, you claim you desperately want to lose weight, but you aren't willing to make any sacrifices. If you seriously want to get off insulin and be healthy, you won't let rush hour traffic keep you from participating."

Arms crossed, Maggie glared at me. "I've lost forty pounds three times before, and it never stays off."

I put a hand on her arm. "It came back because you returned to your old eating habits."

She released a moan. "I've failed so many times before; I guess I don't believe I can do it." She glanced up at me, tears in her eyes. "You really think I can lose this weight and get off insulin?" Her eyes registered a glimmer of hope.

I squeezed her arm. "I know you can, Maggie, but it will take sacrifice, time, and hard work. Just think—you could be fifty pounds lighter by this time next year. Think how much less your knees would ache."

She hesitated, fear etched across her face.

"You can do this, Maggie. I'll help you. Besides, you've got nothing to lose trying."

She glanced up, grinning. "All right, I'll do it."

Thus, every week we weighed ourselves, recorded our food intake, wore pedometers, ate high-protein breakfasts, and explored the emotional triggers behind our overeating. We learned to distract ourselves when tempted to snack.

When Maggie lost three pounds the first week, you'd have thought she'd won an Olympic gold medal. Within a month, she'd lost ten pounds and proudly demonstrated to the group how the waistline of her pants was now loose.

I wanted to cartwheel across the room the week Maggie announced her husband had bought her an exercise bike for Christmas. Now she cycled thirty minutes each morning while watching the *Today* show.

She experienced some setbacks along the way, of course. Three months into the group, Maggie gained two pounds after she pigged out at a family reunion. She hung her head in shame and said nothing during the meeting. Her face, however, said it all: "I'm a failure."

After class, I took her aside. "Maggie, I'm so proud of you."

Her eyes widened. "Proud of me? Why? I ate like a pig and gained two pounds."

"But you showed up tonight, didn't you? That shows you're committed—even when you've messed up. Champions don't quit, they learn from their mistakes. They keep trying until they succeed."

She smirked. "I learned to stay away from the cobbler and ice cream."

I laughed. "You're my star pupil, and you've proven it tonight. You've stayed the course. You may have failed at dieting before, but you're an Honors student now."

In four months, Maggie lost thirty pounds and had already cut her insulin dose by more than half. Her knees no longer ached. When her grandchildren came to visit, she informed me, "I served 'em turkey slices and baby carrots for a snack. They liked 'em just as much as the cookies." She wanted to teach them healthy eating habits, she said.

After she'd lost the thirty pounds with no signs of reverting back to her old eating habits, Maggie announced she was starting a support group at her church. "I want to teach others everything you've taught me. They're all asking me how I've lost my weight."

Everyone applauded and her face beamed. "If I can do it, anybody can. People just need somebody to encourage them along the way."

Amen!

Jennie Ivey would probably be shocked to learn that fifteen "remedial" dieters lost over two hundred pounds of fat because of her story. Amazing what raising the bar on low expectations can do!

"Do not go where the path may lead, go instead where there is no path and leave a trail."

~ RALPH WALDO EMERSON

Caregivers: The Unsung Heroes

As Americans survive heart disease and cancer in record numbers, they often live well into their eighties and nineties. For many, the added longevity comes with a price—the increased incidence of Alzheimer's disease. Statistically, those who live to eighty-five will face a 45 percent risk of developing dementia. Thus, the golden years are called that not because they're so wonderful, but because aging costs a fortune of gold for dental work, pharmacy bills, Poise pads, insurance premiums, and assisted living!

All dressed up without the slightest idea why.

CartoonStock.com

Caring for a spouse or parent with Alzheimer's disease ranks as one of the most thankless and draining jobs imaginable. Patients refuse to bathe or give up the car keys, and they wander the house at all hours of the night. Most parrot the same questions until the spouse wants to run out of the house screaming. Patients can become suspicious and accuse loved ones of stealing their money or misplacing their things. And, of course, they seem to remember nothing they're told. Sadder still, as the disease progresses, they don't seem to know the very loved ones who care for them so tirelessly.

Over the years, I have marveled at the loving care many a wife, husband, or child has provided to a declining family member. Even neighbors and church members pitch in to help. Take Doris and Clarence Smith, for example.

The Smith's celebrated fifty years of marriage together before the first signs of Clarence's mental decline appeared. At first, Doris noticed little things like a botched checking account calculation, a forgotten minister's name, or Clarence leaving the house without his shoes or belt. They joked and called these "senior moments."

When Clarence got lost driving home from a familiar restaurant one night, Doris became more concerned. Soon, he repeated all his stories, refused to bathe, and consistently forgot to zip up his fly.

After a complete medical evaluation, my diagnosis confirmed their worst fears: Alzheimer's. The family was devastated. The loving father and brilliant scientist they'd known was disappearing like steam from a pot of boiling water. He parroted things over and over with a nervous laugh, clueless he'd said the same words five minutes earlier.

Doris took it in stride, though. "He was a wonderful husband and father, and I intend to keep him at home—happy and safe—until the Lord takes him home."

She adjusted her whole life around his illness. She soon discovered if Clarence had routine and stability, he was a relatively easy patient. But if taken to crowded or noisy rooms, he became agitated and uncooperative or would wander away. With time, Doris had to dress him, change his Depends, take him on long car trips to calm him down, and remove the knobs from the stove at night.

After four more years, Clarence quit talking altogether and would sometimes refuse to eat. He stayed wide-awake most of the night and wandered the house, but nodded off during the day. When pushed to stay awake or participate in daytime activities, he became angry and combative. Doris learned not to push him but to wait until he was in a more agreeable mood.

What would make a smart, capable woman like Doris surrender years of her life to perform such thankless, tedious caretaking?

Agape love.

Whitney Houston crooned, "Learning to love yourself, it is the greatest love of all."

I disagree. Love at its deepest level—agape love—is the greatest love of all. Doris gets nothing in return for "babysitting" Clarence 24/7. Their many happy years together buoy her to selfless sacrifice. She continues because Clarence needs her. Trusts her. Loves her. Agape love is deeper than the fleeting passion of eros love that marked their earlier years. It is more self-sacrificing than friendship or philos love. Clarence may not remember her name, but at some visceral level, a bond exists between them that even Alzheimer's cannot destroy.

All around the country selfless spouses and children perform the most basic of tasks, no matter how exhausted they feel.

This story is a tribute to Doris and all the caregivers who have surrendered their lives for those they love. Unsung heroes, all. Your reward is in heaven.

"Things turn out best for those who make the best of the way things turn out."

~ JOHN WOODEN

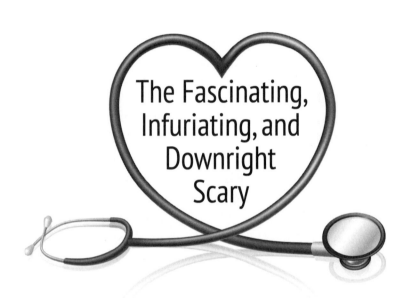

The Fascinating,
Infuriating, and
Downright
Scary

Anorexia Nervosa

I first met Linda, a thirty-two-year-old veterinarian, when she was rushed to the Medical Intensive Care Unit with a dangerously elevated heart rate and a weight of only fifty-two pounds. When her thyroid blood tests came back off the charts high, I thought her emaciation and rapid heart rate were due to severe hyperthyroidism. However, Linda had *intentionally* ingested massive doses of animal thyroid hormone in her desperate effort to lose weight. As a veterinarian, she had ready access to the animal thyroid supplements.

Linda suffered from the worst case of anorexia nervosa I have ever seen. Skinnier than a concentration camp victim, she resisted all inducements to gain weight. In fact, once we'd stabilized Linda's pulse rate, she refused to stay in the hospital, in part because she had no health insurance, and in part because she was solely responsible for a kennel full of sick dogs and cats.

Despite her profound emaciation, none of the reputable eating disorder clinics would take her without health insurance, and no insurance company would accept her due to her pre-existing condition of anorexia nervosa.

Committing her to a mental hospital or eating disorder program against her will was no small task. It required a court order and two physicians to testify she was mentally incompetent. But Linda was competent in every area of her life except weight. A gifted veterinarian, she managed her animal practice, finances, and personal affairs commendably. Thus, legal counselors insisted that since she was an adult, we could not force her into treatment against her will. Talk about delusional! How could she weigh a mere fifty-two pounds and still see herself as fat?

I probed the issue with Linda's mother and discovered the anorexia started at age thirteen when Linda began to develop curves. An older brother uttered a snarky remark that triggered her onto a diet that never quit. The ONLY time Linda's disorder went into remission was during the four years she attended an elite vet school. She became so obsessed with graduating at the top of her class that she transferred all her time and energy into studying instead of exercising and dieting. Unfortunately, as soon as she conquered that hurdle—class valedictorian—she reverted back to her eating disorder with a vengeance and remained that way until the day I met her in the ICU.

Over the next year, I attempted outpatient management with psychiatric meds, but none helped.

THE PROZAC SEEMS TO BE WORKING... LATELY I'M ONLY MILDY INFATUATED WITH COCOA PUFFS...

offthemark.com
ATLANTIC FEATURE © 1998 MARK PARISI

(Most likely because she never took them.) Two psychiatrists consulted on her, but had little to offer; both predicted her case was so severe she would eventually die of her disease. Meanwhile, Linda aimed for a zero fat-gram, eight-hundred-calorie-per-day diet. On top of that, she spent two hours every day power walking.

I wasn't willing to give up on her. I referred her for counseling, twelve-step groups, and parental oversight of her eating, but nothing made a difference.

One day when she came into my office for her bimonthly weighing, a large bag of coins fell out of her underwear onto the floor. She'd wanted to deceive me into thinking she weighed more than she did by hiding the heavy bag of change in her underwear.

After a year of spinning my wheels, with the full support of her family, I jumped through the legal hoops to get her declared mentally incompetent to make her own medical decisions. This granted me the authority to *force* her into an extended inpatient eating disorder program. Since she had finally been approved for TennCare (Tennessee's Medicaid program), finances were no longer an issue, and she could receive the help she needed.

Two days before her scheduled admission, however, she developed a systemic fungal infection called Aspergillosis, and she had to be admitted to the ICU. Because of her suppressed immune system, she was unable to conquer the infection. She died of the infection at the young age of thirty-three, thus fulfilling the dire predictions of her two psychiatrists. While I have no proof, to this day I suspect she intentionally inhaled the *Aspergillus* fungus to delay or avoid admission into the eating disorder clinic. Yes, she was that petrified of gaining weight. As a veterinarian, she had access to the fungus and would be smart enough to know how to inoculate herself.

I look back on Linda's case with profound sadness—a brilliant woman who loved animals but was so bent on self-destruction, no one could help her. Her high intelligence offered no protection against her mental illness, and even two excellent psychiatrists couldn't prevent her untimely demise from the frustrating disorder.

Today, 50 percent of patients with anorexia nervosa can achieve a full remission *if* the disease is caught *early*. The longer a patient waits before aggressive treatment, the poorer the prognosis. Linda had suffered for almost twenty years before she became my patient. Even with the best psychiatric care available, over 15 percent of patients die from the disease and its complications.

"I've exercised by women so thin that buzzards followed them to their cars."

~ ERMA BOMBECK

What About *My* Hair?

I dreaded seeing Mrs. Downer's name on the daily schedule. For twenty years, every office visit, every phone call, she whined, wept, and offered excuses for why she hadn't done a single thing I'd counseled her to do at the last visit. No matter what medication I prescribed, she'd either get some bizarre side effect or claim she couldn't afford it, though she regularly forked out over eight dollars a day for cigarettes. Every visit started the same way:

"How are you today, Mrs. Downer?"

"Oh, I'm in terrible shape." Then she'd plunge into a list of twenty complaints for symptoms that were all self-induced: morning hack (smoking), shortness of breath (smoking and obesity), headaches (non-compliance to her blood pressure

**"This prescription won't make you feel better
but it will stop your whining and make
everyone else feel better."**

medication), knee pain (obesity), bunions (years of narrow, pointy-toed shoes), and fingernail ridges (what did she expect with a diet of Twinkies and Coke?).

One visit, after listening to an hour's worth of complaints, she had the audacity to ask me to code her visit as a "Well-woman exam," because her insurance paid 100 percent for wellness physicals. Well woman, my eye! She hadn't been healthy in decades!

For example: as a consequence of her years of heavy smoking, she developed severe peripheral vascular disease necessitating leg artery surgery. Livid that the doctors and nurses wouldn't give her potent narcotic pain medications in the massive doses she demanded, she stormed out of the hospital against medical advice. Once home, she fell and ripped open all her stitches and even severed an artery. She bled so profusely she required ten pints of blood and emergency surgery.

Next the entire incision dripped with pus from a staph infection, yet she refused to pay the fifty-dollar co-pay to obtain the specific antibiotic her resistant strain of bacteria required. "Can't you give me a four-dollar generic instead?" she demanded. Her poorly controlled diabetes made the infection even worse, and soon gangrene set in, ultimately requiring a below-the-knee amputation.

Did she learn her lesson and quit smoking? Eat better? Take her medications properly? Control her blood sugar? Lose weight? No, no, no, no, and no!

Before long, the artery in her other leg clogged up and necessitated re-vascularization surgery. Since her surgeon was about to leave for a three-week vacation to Europe, her surgery could not be scheduled for over three weeks.

Mrs. Downer whimpered and whined, "I can't possibly wait that long. This pain is excruciating. Unbearable. You've got to do something!" she begged, gripping my hand.

I glanced at her medication sheet. The surgeon had already

prescribed enough pain meds to kill a wooly mammoth. Pleading eyes bore into me. "If you won't help me, just shoot me, or give me an overdose, so I won't have to suffer any more. I can't take it anymore." She wailed and carried on so loudly, no doubt the whole building could hear her.

I called the surgeon's office and explained how miserable she was and how she HAD to have the surgery moved up. I also told them she was making my entire staff miserable with her five-times-a-day phone calls. If my nurse and receptionist were busy, she'd even resorted to calling my billing clerk and begging her to "just shoot me and put me out of my misery."

Turns out, the surgeon's office was barraged with her incessant phone calls as well. In fact, his last receptionist, frazzled from Mrs. Downer's demands, had quit without notice.

To my relief, the surgeon took pity on us all and volunteered to cancel the day he'd taken off to pack and prepare for his vacation. Instead, he would operate on Mrs. Downer. He could perform the surgery the day after tomorrow! I pumped my arm in delight. "Yes!"

We made all the necessary arrangements with the hospital, her insurance company, and anesthesia.

I pranced into her exam room grinning and feeling like a hero. "Wonderful news! Dr. Legpain is so concerned about you that he delayed his vacation a day so he could move up your surgery. He'll operate on you 9:00 a.m. this Thursday, the day after tomorrow. Isn't that fantastic?"

She stared at me blankly then shook her head. "No, I can't do it Thursday. I have a hair appointment. Ten o'clock. On Friday, I've got my manicure, but I could do it Monday. Tell him to make it Monday instead."

No matter how much I tried to explain the surgeon wouldn't delay his vacation five whole days because of a hair appointment, she wouldn't budge. All she would say? "I won't go into the hospital with my hair roots all gray."

When I suggested a walk-in hair salon could dye her hair either today or tomorrow, she shook her head. "No, I don't trust anyone to touch my hair except Cassandra."

Talk about unreasonable! Never had I been so tempted to utter the famous Donald Trump line, "You're fired!"

"Some cause happiness wherever they go; others whenever they go."

~ OSCAR WILDE

Exorcism 101

Perhaps the most frightening case I've ever faced was a woman in the psychiatric ward. I performed comprehensive medical evaluations on psychiatric patients to uncover any conditions that might be contributing to, or even causing, their psychiatric problems. Most patients who were admitted suffered from severe depression or bipolar disease, but a few were overtly psychotic or schizophrenic.

In my medical training, people in the Bible labeled as demon possessed actually suffered from epilepsy, schizophrenia, or profound psychosis, which can now be scientifically explained as chemical or electrical imbalances in the brain. Since modern medications do, for the most part, control these problems, I had little reason to dwell on whether such a thing as demon possession really existed in modern times. I suppose I believed it could happen but that it was exceedingly rare. *I* certainly had

"I don't mind the voices themselves, Doctor. It's the Jersey accents that are driving me nuts."

never encountered anyone truly demon possessed. My luck was about to change.

As I walked into Amanda's room, an eerie and unexplainable chill washed over me. Tortured eyes glared back at me, daring me to touch her. Slash marks and scars covered her wrists, all self-induced, according to the medical record. She wore enough black eyeliner to trump Cleopatra. Large rings and piercings dangled from her ears, eyebrows, lips, nose, and tongue. Her hair—short, spiked, and highlighted with a garish red—was the final touch. Fear inexplicably wrapped around my heart like the serpent tattoos crawling up her arms.

Voice quivering, I asked about her dangerous compulsion to cut herself with razors and knives.

"I hear voices that tell me to do it. They grow stronger and louder until they control me, and I'm powerless to resist." She contorted her hands and added, "They don't let up until I give in and do whatever they tell me to do. Then they go away for a few days."

"What else do these voices tell you to do?" I inquired, attempting to quell my panic.

"They tell me to kill myself because I'm worthless." She picked at a scab on her arm then burst into a hideous, deranged laugh, as though what she'd said was somehow funny.

I shuddered as though I were sitting in the room with Satan himself. As if on cue, her eyes narrowed and she added, "I call the voices 'my little demons' because they totally control me."

My heart pounded, and I suppressed the urge to sprint from the room, never to return. While I had examined and counseled many psychotic and schizophrenic patients, none had triggered such a visceral reaction. With a sudden jolt in my spirit, I felt God tell me this woman was demon possessed.

I'd like to tell you I felt strong and courageous and ready to perform my first exorcism. Instead, my hands and legs shook like a half-chilled bowl of Jell-O. For starters, no "field of pigs" like Jesus had available when He cast out demons was readily available, so where was I supposed to send the little buggers? Would they jump onto me like fleas or bedbugs? I reminded myself of the Scripture, "Greater is He that is in you than he that is in the world." Still, I certainly didn't want the crazed critters spiritually crawling into me!

I reminded myself God wouldn't have revealed to me how this woman was demon possessed if I wasn't supposed to DO something, but I felt incompetent. Could I Google up *How to Perform an Exorcism in Three Easy Steps?* or find an *Exorcism for Dummies* book handy at the nursing station?

The doctor part of me then kicked in with ridiculous concerns. Was there a CPT code for exorcism? Do I make her sign a medical consent? If so, what do I warn her are the risks? Since I'd never performed an exorcism, should I warn her she could end up quacking like a duck or running around in circles like a dog chasing its tail if things went awry? Scenes from *Bewitched*, where Samantha's Aunt Clara bungled up spells and turned people into frogs or goats came to mind. Could she end up hissing and spitting and writhing on the bed like Linda Blair in *The Exorcist*? Wouldn't the nursing staff love that!

Then self-doubt set in. What if God *hadn't* told me she was demon possessed? What if I was just freaking out because of her Goth appearance? If the hospital caught wind of this, would I lose my hospital privileges, be locked up in the psych ward with this crazy woman as my roommate, or lose my medical license? I could picture myself in the hospital president's office trying to justify my actions: "God told me this woman was demon possessed." Right! It sounded like something straight out of a Salem, Massachusetts, witch trial in 1692.

Thus, I was left in a quandary. I could do the sensible thing and ignore my inner prompting and just do the history and physical and get out of Dodge ASAP, or I could take a leap of faith and attempt to help this woman.

I voiced a silent prayer to God. *I don't have any idea what to do, so I could use some help here.*

I started by asking the woman if she *wanted* to be free of her "little demons." She crossed her arms and snapped, "Duh!"

OK, wasn't this going well!

But then she opened up and told me she didn't think they'd ever go away because she'd already tried dozens of medicines and had consulted five different psychiatrists—all without benefit. This actually raised my belief that she might be demon possessed. With modern anti-psychotic medications, most psychotic patients are now able to reach a reasonable level of control, but this woman had clearly not responded to anything. Thus, I had nothing to lose in trying, since nothing else had worked.

I gleaned more history and discovered she once believed in God and even attended church until she was brutally gang-raped in high school. Her internal voices started after she denounced God for not protecting her from the rape. Heavy stuff.

Like the scales falling from Paul's eyes, I now saw this woman not as a terrifying demonized freak, but as a wounded soul needing spiritual healing. While not a Catholic priest, I decided to try and expel the demons. Even if she *wasn't* demon possessed, and I had just spooked myself out because of her frightening appearance, I could do no harm by praying for her. Nor would praying silently over her while examining her heart and lungs violate any hospital rules.

As I performed her exam, I laid a hand on her and silently commanded the demons to leave and to never return in the name of Jesus, through the power of the Holy Spirit. I prayed and begged God to release this woman from bondage. Feeling more confident and sensing openness from Amanda, I asked if she would like me to pray with her, and she nodded, tears in her eyes. Afterwards, I provided the name of several excellent churches near her apartment that she could attend, and I encouraged her to read the Bible and pray daily. I wrote down several scriptures she should memorize and say to her "little demons" if they ever returned to taunt her. When I left, her demonic, crazed glare was gone, and she even gave me a hug and thanked me. The next day, I brought her a Bible. I had highlighted key verses for her to memorize and use in spiritual warfare against any future demonic attacks.

She was released from the hospital four days later, supposedly cured by her new anti-psychotic drug, Clozaril. The voices were gone! Since I never heard from the woman again, I'll never know if it was my half-baked exorcism attempt or the new antipsychotic that made the difference. Either way, I'm glad she's better. I have never seen using medication as lacking faith, or praying for healing as unscientific. Why not use every tool possible to promote healing?

"For God has not given us the spirit of fear; but of power, and of love, and of a sound mind."

~ 2 TIMOTHY 1:7 (NEW KJV)

The Good, the Bad, and the Stolen

Over the years, patients have bestowed wonderful, thoughtful gifts to my staff and me. One patient hand-crocheted a soft blue receiving blanket when my son was born. Several patients whipped up gourmet lunches—a welcome diversion from my usual boring carton of fat-free yogurt. An especially crafty patient hand-designed a tote bag out of old neckties. Handmade beaded earrings and bracelets, silk scarves, pots of impossible-to-find coleuses, a rare canary-yellow orchid, and a hand-carved wooden salad bowl—the list goes on and on.

At Christmastime our office smells like a bakery, thanks to all the goodies patients concoct for us. In the summer, we gorge on the plump, juicy tomatoes, succulent squash, eggplants, yams, and cucumbers our gardener patients provide. Considering I've forgotten my best friend's birthday for ten years running, the thoughtfulness and generosity of my patients never ceases to amaze me.

A few gifts, however, weren't so nice. Good ol' Bob offered me a floor-to-ceiling plastic letter holder he'd purchased at a yard sale for fifty cents, only to discover the thing was too

"Nice iron. Your wife will love it. While I wrap it, you might want to go over to sporting goods and pick out a helmet."

tall for his trailer! "It's a little dirty and has a big crack, but it's still usable," he insisted. Another time, Bob tried to unload one of his five mangy cats. I declined when I learned the cat was in serious need of an urologist, as it piddled all over his trailer. That's why he wanted to get rid of it!

One woman graced me with the videotape of her gallbladder surgery. She even had the movie displayed in a gift bag, complete with tissue paper and ribbons. "You'll love watching this, since you're a medical person," she enthused.

Seriously? Forget *Downton Abbey*. Forget *Pride and Prejudice*. Just sit me down with a big bowl of popcorn and . . . *a gallbladder surgery?* News flash: even nerdy doctors don't watch videos of gall bladder surgery for Friday-night entertainment!

Plus, if I liked blood and gore, I'd have become a surgeon. We internists accuse surgeons of being butchers, and surgeons accuse us internists of sitting around contemplating our navels when we could instead cut something out and save a life. It reminds me of the humorous saying that *specialists learn more and more about less and less until they know everything about nothing, while general practitioners know less and less about more and more until they know nothing about everything.*

I've digressed! Back to gifts!

The other gift I will never forget is an ornate Christmas vest from an expensive department store, complete with matching turtleneck and darling little reindeer earrings. What an expensive gift from a woman living on just a disability check. I felt touched that she valued my doctoring enough to purchase such a pricey gift on her limited salary. As I held up the adorable reindeer vest, I oohed and aahed. "Martha, you shouldn't have."

Turns out, she didn't! She stole it! Unbeknownst to me, Martha was a kleptomaniac who was later caught shoplifting clothes from the very same department store from which my vest came! I found out about her stealing problem when she called me several months later wanting an official letter claiming the

anti-depressant I'd prescribed had *made* her steal it. With that reasoning, can I claim my vitamin D supplement made me devour that last bowl of French Silk ice cream?

Mr. Gibson wins the award for the *worst* Christmas gifts ever— even worse than the Betsy doll I received for my sixth birthday.

He marched into my office shortly before Christmas one year with gifts for my entire staff. His treasure trove included cheap, bendable plastic combs and tiny bars of soap emblazoned with the logo of a local motel. One staff member received a plastic hospital razor guaranteed to hack out a sizeable chunk of her leg every time she shaved. Another received a toothbrush with bent bristles and even a speck of toothpaste in it. I got the mother lode of gifts: a pink plastic vomit basin! (Please tell me he hadn't used it before, as well!)

He obtained his gifts during a recent hospital stay. I know this because the nurse paged me one night to inquire why Mr. Gibson kept requesting new toiletry kits. "He's bald, has a beard, and wears dentures. What's he doing with all those combs and razors and toothbrushes?"

What indeed! Re-gifting!

"Go ahead and re-gift. It's not like you were going to give them something thoughtful or useful, anyway."

~ JERRY SEINFELD

Fatal Demise

Margaret, a seventy-year-old with dangerously high blood pressure, had failed with every hypertensive medication I had ever prescribed. One made her gain weight (the cookies and ice cream had nothing to do with it), she claimed. Another made her tired. A third caused hair thinning, and the fourth made her teeth hurt. (Never mind that her mouth was full of decaying teeth.)

I pointed out that mildly thinning hair beat a massive stroke, but my pep talk did no good. She refused to take the medicine, and I was forced to prescribe yet another drug for her hypertension.

Not surprisingly, a month later, Margaret showed up for her appointment with a blood pressure of 210/115.

"Are you taking that new blood pressure medication I prescribed?"

Margaret scowled and pulled the package insert for lisinopril out of her purse. She handed it to me and pointed accus-

"I don't care which doctor I see. I'm not going to listen to him anyway."

ingly to the paragraph she'd highlighted in yellow. "No. You prescribe me a drug that causes fatal demise. Are you *trying* to kill me?"

Fatal demise? What was she talking about?

I skimmed her highlighted handout and had to bite the inside of my cheeks to keep from laughing. It didn't say "*fatal*" demise—it said "*fetal*" demise, *if used by a woman in her second trimester of pregnancy.* At age seventy, she was hardly at risk for pregnancy! When I told her this, she crossed her arms and sputtered, "If that drug can kill teeny-tiny babies, I ain't taking it." She glared at me like I'd prescribed strychnine. Apparently, she'd rather keel over with a coronary.

Another time, shortly after her husband died, Margaret had trouble falling asleep and had requested something "mild" to help her out. I prescribed a month's worth of the lowest dose of a weak sleeping pill. The next day, she called the office to inform me she would NOT be taking "that dangerous drug" I'd prescribed.

What?

Did I know, she demanded, that according to the package insert, if she took *eighteen* of them all at one time, it could *kill* her? Why was I prescribing such a dangerous drug?

When I pointed out she was only supposed to take *one* pill, and not *eighteen*, she sputtered, "if that drug can kill me, I ain't taking it."

Fine! If she got tired enough, she'd eventually fall asleep!

> *"Be careful about reading health books—*
> *you may die of a misprint."*
>
> ~ MARK TWAIN

The Worst Patient Ever

I'll never forget Willie Williams, my worst patient ever: always late or no-showing for appointments, non-compliant with his medications, rude and unreasonable with my staff. I mentally threatened to dismiss him from my practice every December— as a Christmas gift to myself!

As always, Willie dragged in forty minutes late for today's visit, but then had the nerve to cuss out my receptionist after *he'd* waited a mere ten minutes for me.

Once back in the exam room with me, he flopped open a folder crammed with information about three new herbal treatments he'd read about online that worked more "natural-like" than the medicines I'd prescribed.

I'm not against natural or holistic treatments, *if they work,* but Willie had forked out, yet again, sixty dollars for some all-natural, "miracle" herb supposedly out of Bolivia that hadn't lowered his blood pressure any better than a jug full of earwax. Nonetheless, Willie pitched a fit that the medication I prescribed, which had a proven efficacy and safety record with the FDA, cost twenty-five dollars a month! "Those drug companies are nothing but a pack of %&@$ robbers! Thieves, all of them."

I pointed out that the CEO of the herbal company Willie had coughed up sixty dollars to for an herb that hadn't lowered his blood pressure one iota was also no doubt laughing his way to the bank.

Willie's hands fisted. "My pressure's up because that &%*$ receptionist of yours got all snippy with me when I didn't have my office co-pay today. She's nothing but a greedy battle-axe." Index finger in my face, he shouted, "You ought to fire the uppity broad."

*I ought to fire **you**, Willie.*

With his fist only two inches from my nose, I kept my opinion to myself.

He then went off on a tirade about uppity receptionists and greedy doctors always wanting money for office co-pays.

Since Willie *never* paid his co-pay and currently owed me more than *ninety* dollars in unpaid co-pays, I felt unfairly attacked. Most doctors would have dismissed him years ago. Triggered by his ingratitude, I pointed out, "Perhaps if you didn't waste your money on cigarettes, beer, and ineffective herbs from Bolivia, you could *afford* your office co-pays."

That went over big.

His face turned crimson, his hands fisted, and I thought a knuckle sandwich would soon replace my fat-free yogurt for lunch. "Dr. Burbank, in all the years I've been alive, you're the WORST doctor I've ever had."

Gee, thanks a bunch!

I shouldn't have said it, but I couldn't resist. "Oh, yeah? Well, out of the *ten thousand* patients I've doctored in the last twenty-five years, you rank dead last. If you think I'm such a rotten doctor, find yourself a new one."

I stormed out of the room, no doubt needing a hypertension medicine myself! And not

"Call me that one more time and you can find yourself another doctor!"

one from Bolivia!

Never had I lost my temper with a patient before, but Willie had gotten under my skin! I shook my head, still in shock I'd behaved in such a childish, unprofessional manner. Truth be told, however, I wanted to dance around the room in glee. As Martin Luther King Jr. once said, "Free at last! Free at last! Thank God Almighty, we are free at last!"

"I did not attend his funeral, but I sent a nice letter saying I approved of it."

~ MARK TWAIN

Tornado

Tornado warnings echo across Nashville every spring, yet in the twelve years I'd lived in Nashville, I'd never seen one. Thus, when the weatherman doled out dire predictions for a huge twister in April of 1998, I rolled my eyes. No doubt another Peter (the weatherman) crying wolf again and a lot of hoopla over nothing.

Just in case, however, I asked the mother of one of my staff members to stay glued to her television screen and call us at the earliest sign of a tornado heading our way.

If such an emergency arose, I'd evacuate patients from my sixth floor office to the basement with the professionalism of Rudy Giuliani. A heroine in the midst of crisis, a tower of strength, I'd be.

Meanwhile, a nasty storm pummeled buckets of rain at the large picture windows in my office. Terri, our resident tornado expert—based solely on her years of living in Oklahoma—eyed the ominous gray cloud swirling outside the office. "We need to move the patients to the basement now," she said as worry lines etched her forehead.

After eyeing the mile-wide gray cloud, I shrugged; it didn't look like the funnel cloud that flung Dorothy and Toto to the Land of Oz, so I was unconvinced. "It's probably just a big thunder cloud," I said, suspecting she was secretly trying to weasel out of patient callbacks. "Besides, Cathy's mother promised to call us *with plenty of notice*. We're fine," I insisted, pushing her in the direction of the Mount Everest of paperwork on her desk.

Suddenly, Cathy's mother called and hollered into the phone, "Get to the basement—NOW! It's hit Centennial Park, and it's heading your way. Hurry, or you're all gonna die!" Now sobbing, she screamed, "RUN FOR YOUR LIVES!"

So much for plenty of notice and my calm, professional evacuation!

I ran around the office shrieking like a banshee on cocaine for everyone to hightail it to the basement. NOW! I felt like Sargent Carter screaming at Gomer Pyle.

The howling wind intensified, and the twister swirled ever closer. An ominous crack snaked its way down the massive picture window in my office.

Two pitiful patients had to escape to the basement clad only in paper gowns. They strove—unsuccessfully—to cover their bottoms and bosoms with the clothes they carried.

I shoved everyone toward the elevator. "No, you don't have time to re-dress." "There's no time to go to the bathroom." And my favorite, *"Forget the lipstick!"*

Just as we entered the elevator, the power died. Great! Where was rescuing an office full of half-naked people in the job description of a doctor? This ranked right up there with cleaning feces off the patient commode.

I pointed in the direction of the stairwell, and the patients began hightailing it down six flights of stairs. Meanwhile, I could hear the strong wind blustering outside. The windows rattled as though convulsing in an epileptic fit. My heart pounded as all rational thought swirled away.

I'm not cut out for this knight-in-shining-armor stuff; if I'd wanted to run into burning buildings, I'd have become a fireman. I felt like the Cowardly Lion clutching his tail and chanting, "I do believe in spooks. I do believe in spooks."

Just as I was about to dash down the stairs myself, I noticed one of my oldest—and heaviest—patients sitting in a wheelchair. Her son had dropped her off and left. She was supposed to call him when ready for a ride home. Swell!

What was I supposed to do with her?

Since she weighed twice my weight, I couldn't carry her down the stairs. Panic overtook me. How was I supposed to rescue her when I was falling apart at the seams myself?

I have to confess my first—and decidedly uncharitable— thought was to just leave her there. She'd already lived a long life, while I still had two little kids at home who needed their mother. If my conscience hadn't convicted me, I might well have abandoned her and dashed down the stairs to save my own hide.

No point in both of us dying, right?

I stuffed the selfish thought and pushed her wheelchair to the stairs. With the help of three men, we thump, thump, thumped her wheelchair down the six flights of stairs while she sputtered and cursed and shrieked at us to go easy on her bad back. Nerves fried, I nearly snapped, "Zip it, lady! *We're* gonna have bad backs, too, after lugging you down all these stairs."

We were sequestered to the basement for two long hours as multiple twisters tore through Nashville. I was a mental wreck, as I hadn't heard a word from my husband who was picking up our children from school at the very time the tornadoes ripped through Nashville. Even worse, my in-laws were camped in a trailer right in the tornado's path. Were they okay? The responsibility of evacuating patients while hearing on the radio about devastation all over Nashville sucked the life out of me. I just wanted to go home and hug my family—if they were alive.

Once given the green light to leave the basement, the lady in the wheelchair insisted, "I didn't come here today to be thrown down the stairs like some dog toy. I need this ear checked out."

She tugged at her ear. "It hurts like the dickens, and I'm not leaving 'til you check it."

Thankfully, the emergency generator had kicked in, so the elevators worked. I wheeled her back to my office. Unfortunately, the generator did *not* provide power in my exam rooms. Thus, my otoscope didn't light up. Her ear canal was pitch black; I couldn't see a thing.

No way did I want to tell this crotchety old woman she'd withstood a tornado, a bumpy ride down six flights of stairs, and a two-hour wait in a dank basement for nothing. Frankly, I was too drained to face her wrath.

Thus, I peered into her ear with my useless otoscope and I remarked, "I bet that ear really hurts." Since I couldn't tell if she had an infection, I erred on the side of caution and prescribed amoxicillin. "See me in ten days if it's not better."

Praise God, my family and home survived unscathed. Nashville? Not so much! Andrew Jackson's homestead (called the Hermitage), St. Ann's Episcopal Church, a hospital daycare just a half-mile from my office, six hundred businesses, and three hundred homes were damaged or destroyed—more than a hundred million dollars' worth of damage.

Never again will I blow off tornado warnings. In fact, if Terri insists a twister is heading our way, I'll race her to the basement!

"It's not that I'm afraid to die—
I just don't want to be there when it happens."

~ WOODY ALLEN

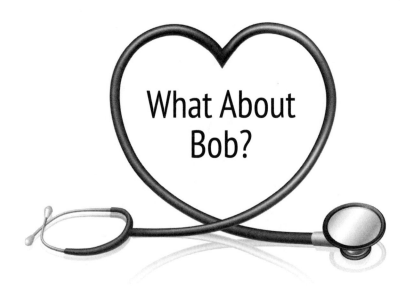

What About
Bob?

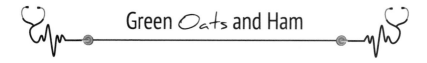

Green Oats and Ham

Ever known someone with the IQ of a bathroom plunger? Well, that pretty much sums up Bob's mental acuity.

One day, after he'd asked my receptionist a particularly stupid question, she muttered, "That man is dumber than a squashed zucchini."

While I agreed with her, I halfheartedly reprimanded her. After all, Bob couldn't help if he had more toe jam than brains. Admittedly, he did drive my staff and me crazy. How he managed to keep a full-time job as a construction worker when he couldn't grasp the simplest of medical concepts never ceased to amaze me.

One day, when his blood cholesterol came back at 246 mg/dl, (normal is less than 200 mg/dl), my nurse reviewed the basics of a low-cholesterol diet: eat more fruits and vegetables, more salmon, chicken, almonds, whole grains, and use olive oil. Eat less greasy red meat, cheese, and fried foods. Simple, right?

Wrong! From that day forward, Bob called every day with such inane questions as

"Is oatmeal considered a fried food?" Now I know they fry a lot of foods in the South that we'd never fry back in my home state of Vermont (think turkeys, green tomatoes, and ice cream), but to my knowledge, even Southerners didn't fry oatmeal!

Another day, he asked, "If I grill a hamburger until it's totally black, is it still considered a red meat?"

One hectic day when Bob had already called multiple times, my harried receptionist got frustrated with him and snapped, "Just eat more salmon, apples, chicken, carrots, and spinach. Eat more oatmeal and broccoli." With the phone ringing off the hook, she added, "I need to go now, Bob. Bye." Click.

Imagine my shock when a month later, Bob called to ask if I had any other brilliant ideas for his breakfast menu besides oatmeal and broccoli. Turns out, he had cooked up a pan of oatmeal with broccoli in it every single morning for the last month! "Green oatmeal ain't very appetizin'," he lamented. "And it don't taste that great, either."

You think? I had to chomp on the inside of my cheeks to keep from laughing at the image of him facing his bowl of green broccoli oatmeal every morning for thirty days straight.

I then opened his eyes to the wonders of Egg Beaters, whole-wheat English muffins with natural peanut butter, low-fat yogurt, and Cheerios with skim milk.

"As a child my family's menu consisted of two choices: take it or leave it."

~ BUDDY HACKETT

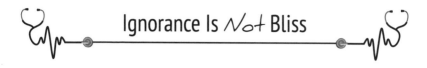

Ignorance Is *Not* Bliss

At almost every visit to our office, Bob embarrasses himself or my staff. When he came in for his last physical, he was handed a one-page Review of Systems form to complete while sitting in the waiting room. The Review of Systems form lists dozens of symptoms from headache to constipation to ingrown toenails. The patient circles any symptoms he or she may endure so we can discuss them during the office visit.

Ten minutes after receiving his form, Bob strolled up to my receptionist and said loud enough for the entire waiting room to hear, "What is imPOtency? I-M-P-O-T-E-N-C-Y?" Yes, he even spelled it out loud for her in his booming voice, lest anyone in the waiting room missed it the first time.

My receptionist turned fifty shades of red before responding, "Bob, if you have to ask what it is, you probably don't have it."

The real and somewhat embarrassing cause of the mass extinction ... reptile dysfunction.

By permission of Leigh Rubin and Creators Syndicate, Inc.

Not taking the hint, Bob said, "But I don't know if I have it or not. Do *you* know if I have imPOtency?"

By this time, every patient in the waiting room was smirking and snickering and elbowing each other, all watching to see how my usually unflappable receptionist would handle the question.

Without missing a beat she said, "Bob, I definitely *don't* know, nor do I *want* to know." She then added, "Why don't you discuss this with Dr. Burbank *privately*, when you're back in the exam room."

Never one to pick up on social cues, Bob began asking the patients in the waiting room if any of *them* knew what imPOtency was. Meanwhile, my receptionist dashed to the back, snatched my nurse by the scruff of the neck, and threatened bodily harm if she didn't bring Bob back to an exam room *NOW*, before the patients in the waiting room fled the office in droves.

Once escorted back to the exam room, I explained to Bob what IMpotency meant. He laughed and volunteered, "Naw, I don't have that. I do just fine with the ladies, know what I mean?" Snort, snort.

Okay, too much information. Like my receptionist, I didn't know, nor did I *want* to know!

Bob then added, "You ought to clue in your receptionist and them other folks in the waiting room. None of them knew what the word meant either!"

"He fell out of the stupid tree and hit every branch on the way down!"

~AUTHOR UNKNOWN

A Phone Call I'd Rather Forget

B ob had somehow managed to find himself a woman. Unfortunately, I found out about the relationship in the most tasteless manner imaginable.

I was hosting a dinner party for friends and was about to serve the chocolate éclair dessert when my pager buzzed. I checked the number and groaned. Bob. (Because of all his inane phone calls about his low-cholesterol diet, I'd memorized his home, work, and cell phone numbers.) Knowing Bob would likely tie me up for a good fifteen minutes, I asked my husband to serve the dessert while I tackled the phone call.

"How can I help you, Bob?"

"Uh, Dr. Burbank, Irene here wants to ask you a question."

He must have handed her the phone because the next thing I heard was the gravelly voice of a chain smoker. Mincing no words, she went straight for the jugular. "What's the matter with this guy?"

Startled, I said, "I beg your pardon? Of course, I knew what was the matter with Bob—he was dumber than a squashed zucchini—but I could hardly say that with him standing next to her! So I hedged. "What exactly do you mean?"

"I mean, he can't get it up," she snapped with a disgusted tone.

Hmm—maybe Bob did suffer I-M-P-O-T-E-N-C-Y after all. What man wouldn't with this insensitive broad?

She continued her rant. "We met at the bar tonight, and he seemed okay, so I invited him to my apartment. But the guy can't get it up. I want you to fix him, or I got no use for him."

Wasn't she a charmer! Bob sure knew how to pick 'em.

Since I knew from his recent physical he didn't normally

have trouble sexually, I concluded this woman's demanding and demeaning approach would render any man impotent. Plus, they'd just met!

I informed her men often needed time to relax and feel comfortable with a new partner. Perhaps they should get to know each other better before attempting intimacy. "Give the relationship more time," I suggested.

"How much more time is he gonna need?" she sputtered. "We've already been at it for an hour."

I rolled my eyes. Even a hooker would show more sensitivity!

Bob must have taken the phone back because the next voice I heard was his. "I think you're right, Dr. Burbank. I think Irene being twenty years older than me is weirding me out. I mean she don't look *that* bad for an old lady. She's saggy, wrinkled, and droopy, but probably no worse than any other woman pushing seventy."

I couldn't believe my ears! Which of the two needed sensitivity training more? Maybe they deserved each other! I wanted to tell her, "Look lady, he's dumb. Trust me, you don't want him." I wanted to tell Bob, "She doesn't care two cents about you. She's nothing but a sleaze bucket. Be grateful you *couldn't* perform, or she'd likely have landed you in an STD clinic."

I stuffed my harsh thoughts and pointed out the relationship didn't seem to be working out. Perhaps they should call it a night. They both heartily agreed and ended the call.

I hung up the phone, still shaking my head in disbelief. In fact, the thought of the two of them in bed together sickened me so much I couldn't stomach the thought of eating my dessert!

Are You a Rat, Bob?

Two in the morning, and my pager beeped. I groped around my nightstand for my reading glasses, beeper, and a flashlight. I recognized the phone number displayed on my beeper and moaned. Bob. Not again! I prayed this conversation would be less tawdry than the one I'd had after his bar pickup.

I dialed the number and braced myself for who knows what. "Ahh, Dr. Burbank? This is Bob."

I attempted to stuff my surly attitude and feigned as pleasant a voice as I could muster at two in the morning. "How can I help you, Bob?"

"I want the name of a new neurologist."

He woke me up for that? Why couldn't he have waited until morning, when the office opened? I clenched my teeth in disgust, my night of restful sleep ruined by such a flimsy reason. Then my conscience clobbered me.

You are called to be kind, even with the dim-witted.

I forced myself to change my attitude. "Why do you want a new neurologist, Bob? Dr. Brainer is one of the best in the city."

"I don't like him no more," he sputtered with a petulant tone. "He's got a bee up his butt."

Oh, brother! I switched the phone to my other ear. "What happened, Bob?"

"All's I did was call him up tonight to ask one simple question. He jumped all over me a-yellin' and a-hollerin' and a-screamin' that I ain't got no business waking up a doctor in the middle of the night just to ask a question that could have waited until morning. Said I shouldn't be callin' unless it's an emergency."

Guess he didn't get the message since he woke me up just to complain about his neurologist!

On and on he ranted. "I just wanted to ask about that new

seizure drug they mentioned on the news last night. Wondered if it would be good for me."

"No, seriously. I'm in medicine. Cutting edge stuff. I work in a lab downtown."

I took a huge breath and counted to ten to keep myself from a-yellin' and a-hollerin' and a-screamin' at him. "First of all, Bob, the drug has only been tried on *laboratory animals*. It hasn't even been tested on humans. It's not FDA approved."

"But they said the drug looked promising and . . . "

I interrupted. *"In laboratory animals. Are you a rat, Bob?"* (I have to go simple with Bob.)

He laughed. "No."

"Then I wouldn't take it. Besides, why would you want to change medications? You haven't had a seizure in years, and your epilepsy's in great control."

"Yeah, but I thought I might like to try somethin' new."

Something new? Like a new flavor of ice cream or a new haircut? How about a new brain—one that knows enough not to wake up two doctors in the middle of the night to ask about a seizure drug that's only been tested in rats!

"We live in an era of smart phones and stupid people."

~AUTHOR UNKNOWN

Bob's Embarrassing Pharmacy Encounter

After being completely humiliated by his geriatric strumpet, Bob came in and admitted he was now having some trouble with his new girlfriend and demanded I prescribe him "that there Viagra drug" he'd heard about on television. With decided misgivings and guilt, I reviewed the possible side effects of the drug and strongly encouraged consistent condom use. God forbid he pass his genes on to another generation. I told Bob the drug should be taken one hour before relations. Bob folded the prescription and stuffed it into his pants pocket.

He raced to the pharmacy. Too embarrassed for anyone to see what the script was for, he slid it across the pharmacy counter upside down and pushed it toward the pharmacist, making a studied effort to avoid eye contact.

Bob told me later the pharmacist glanced at the script and smirked at him like they were sharing an inside joke. The pharmacist, bespectacled and bald, told Bob to browse around the store. "I'll page you when your script is ready."

Twenty minutes later, the following announcement was broadcast overhead for shoppers everywhere to hear: "Will the patient with the Viagra prescription please come to the pharmacy—your prescription is now ready."

Shamefaced, Bob slunk to the counter, noticing several shoppers smirking and staring at him. "Did you have to announce it over the loudspeaker?" he hissed at the pharmacist. "I don't want nobody knowin' I take this stuff."

The pharmacist adjusted his glasses. "HIPAA law no longer allows us to announce the patient's name overhead, so we now page by the name of the medication." The pharmacist seemed unapologetic. He then reviewed the potential side effects in a voice loud enough to educate shoppers three aisles over.

When the pharmacist got to the side effect of an erection lasting longer than four hours, Bob grinned. "Four hours? Won't my girlfriend love that!"

The pharmacist turned green.

Later that night, Bob decided to try Viagra for the first time and swallowed his first pill.

One hour later Bob paged me. "Uh, Dr. Burbank? That there Viagra don't work. I took it an hour ago and it ain't done squat."

What was that I heard playing in the background—*a boxing match?* "Where are you, Bob?" I inquired.

"I'm home. Watching a boxing match on TV."

How's that for setting a romantic mood? "Bob, maybe if you and your girlfriend did something a little more romantic than watching boxing—that would help."

"Oh, she ain't here yet. It's just Trixie and me." (Trixie is his vicious Siamese guard cat.)

"You mean your girlfriend isn't even in the room? Viagra doesn't just pump you up like a bicycle tire pump. You have to

"I told you to go easy on the viagra!"

engage in normal sexual activity. Foreplay."

Bob probably hadn't a clue what the word meant.

He released a nervous laugh. "Oh! The pharmacist didn't tell me that. I figured I'd wait for it to work, and then I'd head on over to Trina's trailer. I figured when she saw how excited I was, she'd be begging me for some action—know what I mean?" He laughed so hard he snorted.

Eeww and double eeww! Was it too late to rescind his prescription?

Was Bob's idea of an aphrodisiac watching one guy walloping another in the head with a boxing glove?

"Love is an irresistible desire to be irresistibly desired."

~ ROBERT FROST

Bob's Home Security System

B ob responded to an advertisement for a free home security installation. My first thought? What did Bob own in his
dilapidated trailer that anyone would *want* to steal? One of his
five mangy, piddling cats? His filthy cat box? His *Playboy* magazines?

When the salesman arrived at Bob's trailer to set up the system, he first wanted Bob to sign a one-year service agreement
for the low monthly rate of $19.95.

Bob accused the man of false advertising and threatened
to sue him. After all, Bob warned, "I am a second cousin to
former Congressman Thomas Schlepper, so I have power in
high places." I'll bet the congressman cringed every time Bob

"I ALREADY HAVE A HOME SECURITY SYSTEM."

bragged publicly that he was a kinfolk. Perhaps that explains Congressman Schlepper's poor showing in his last reelection bid.

Bob sputtered, "It ain't free if he expects me to pay $19.95 a month to keep it going! What good is a security system that ain't activated? That thar's false advertising. I've got a good mind to report him to Cousin Tom."

I did agree with Bob that the company's advertising was a bit misleading.

Then Bob added the clincher. "Besides, I don't need no high-falutin' security system. I got me a baseball bat sitting right near the front door. And if that fails, I got me a loaded rifle under the bed. And if that fails, Trixie (his mean, mangy Siamese cat) will hiss, bite, and scratch anyone who comes into the trailer. She's my guard cat."

Hmmm. Remind me never to make a house call on Bob.

Bob should post a sign in his yard warning intruders stating: **Warning: trailer guarded with a baseball bat, rifle, and vicious Siamese.**

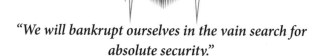

"We will bankrupt ourselves in the vain search for absolute security."

~ DWIGHT D. EISENHOWER

Homeland Security's
Newest Recruit

One day, Bob decided his guard cat, Trixie, would make a stellar addition to the Department of Homeland Security. "They use dogs to sniff out drugs and bombs, why not cats?"

Bob got a seamstress friend to design a bright yellow cat sweater appliqued with bold letters that read, "Department of Homeland Security." When he added black knitted booties and a tri-cornered black felt hat, Trixie was dressed to the nine (lives, that is.).

If you can believe it, Bob actually brought Trixie, decked out in her yellow sweater, hat, and booties, to the airport to meet with the head of security, where he volunteered the services of Trixie for our airport's security.

Of course, the head honcho had no idea Bob was serious. He

"HAVE BUDGET CUTS REDUCED US TO THIS?"

laughed, patted Bob on the back, and complimented him on the hilarious cat outfit. Thankfully, he knew enough *not* to pat the yowling, hissing beast; no doubt Trixie's already ill-tempered disposition was only made worse after enduring the public humiliation of wearing such a ridiculous get-up.

Since airport security wouldn't take Trixie, Bob brought her to his local police precinct. Surely they would jump at the chance for a free security cat. "I wasn't gonna charge 'em or anything. I just thought Trixie could be taught to sniff out them illegal drugs, like dogs do."

Right! Just what every police precinct needs—a yowling, hissing, piddling, scratching, cantankerous feline! Needless to say, the police chief politely declined Bob's offer by claiming several of his officers were allergic to cats.

When Bob offered to bring Trixie into my medical office so patients could ooh and ahh over her new outfit, I convinced him to bring pictures instead. I didn't think OSHA would approve of a vicious cat prowling around the office!

"Thousands of years ago, cats were worshipped as gods. Cats have never forgotten this."

~Author unknown

*Sadly, good old "Bob" died in a car wreck a few years back.
He left behind no spouse, children, or living family members
to embarrass by publishing his story.*

Miracles and
Divine
Intervention

Not Until She Graduates

One of the privileges of practicing medicine is witnessing miracles firsthand. I've given up trying to figure out when and for whom God will intervene, but when He does, I am always left awestruck, and my faith is strengthened. Take Patricia Baxter, for example.

A pleasant forty-seven-year-old librarian, she took delight in mothering her bubbly fifteen-year-old daughter, Julie. Since Patricia and her husband had struggled with infertility for years before conceiving, they savored every moment with their daughter. At her annual check-ups, Patricia displayed photos of Julie singing in the church choir, or kicking the winning soccer goal, or decorating a lopsided birthday cake she had baked for her father. In fact, Patricia was more interested in talking about her daughter than complaining about her creaky knee or ten-pound weight gain like so many women her age.

One year, however, Patricia mentioned unexplained severe fatigue, nosebleeds, easy bruising, and chronic sinus infections. A battery of tests confirmed my suspicion: acute leukemia. The leukemia cells—called blasts—had crowded out the healthy cells in her bone marrow, leading to bleeding, anemia, and fatigue.

I referred her to a top oncologist, and she began the first of six cycles of chemotherapy. Hair loss, nausea, exhaustion, and frequent blood transfusions became her constant companions.

Because of Julie, Patricia was desperate to live. So desperate, she probably would have snuck into Mexico at the bottom of an avocado truck to obtain illegal Laetrile if she'd thought it would cure her leukemia. She and Julie did everything together: Girl Scouts, shopping, church choir, cooking, and you name it. Thus, they had never suffered the "you've-ruined-my-life; I-hate-you, Mom," drama so many teenage girls and mothers weather. Leaving Julie to fend for herself during her tumultuous teen years was unthinkable.

One day, after a rough cycle of chemotherapy, Patricia gripped my hand and pleaded, "Please pray for me that this chemotherapy works and God allows me to see Julie graduate from high school. I don't need to grow old; I just don't want to abandon Julie when she needs me the most. I just want to see her graduate from high school. Is three years too much to ask for?"

Tears filled my eyes. As a mother of two children myself, I could share her desire to usher her daughter into adulthood. What if my daughter had to face life with no mom? With a hand on Patricia's shoulder, I promised, "I will pray for you every day, and I'll get my staff and prayer group to pray also."

The creases in her face relaxed. "Thank you," she whispered, squeezing my hand. "All we can do is pray. The rest is in God's hands."

We thought our prayers were answered when the blasts dis-

glasbergen.com

"I saw the bright light and the tunnel, but they sent me back because I haven't paid off my student loans."

appeared and her blood counts normalized, and she seemed to be responding to the chemotherapy. But after her fifth cycle, the blasts returned, and her blood counts plummeted; her leukemia had returned with a vengeance, and it was now resistant to chemotherapy.

"We'll try a different drug," her oncologist reassured her, but it, too, proved a failure. Patricia then agreed to participate in an experimental drug trial, but the drug caused a severe rash and painful mouth sores. Worse yet, it didn't work. Unfortunately, no one in her family was a match for a bone marrow transplant. Patricia was out of luck.

With leukemia hogging her bone marrow, she required blood and platelet transfusions almost daily until she developed antibodies to the transfused platelets and destroyed them within hours. Her prognosis looked bleak.

Patricia had unwavering faith, though. Along with her family, church, friends, and doctors, she prayed for a miracle. Her one persistent prayer? "Let me live to see Julie graduate from high school."

Infections and nosebleeds necessitating trips to the hospital now plagued her. One night, disaster struck: she hemorrhaged into her lungs and brain. Paramedics rushed her to the ER. She was already comatose and required a ventilator. Things looked so hopeless the hematologist called in her family to say their final goodbyes. "She won't survive the night," he told them sadly. A "Do Not Resuscitate" order was added to her chart in defeat.

Later that night, I stopped by her room wishing and praying I could do something. I poured over her chart and shook my head. I placed a hand on her shoulder and offered up a last heartfelt plea. "God, I pray for a miracle. Patricia just wants to see her daughter finish high school. If it is Your will, please grant her that."

I exited her room suspecting this would be the last time I'd see her this side of heaven. My eyes pooled, as I'd grown fond of Patricia and her family. *Why, God? Why Patricia? Her family needs her.*

Miraculously, Patricia survived the night, and over the next few days, with no treatment whatsoever, her platelet count increased. Soon, the blasts were gone! My mouth dropped in shock. *What's going on?* Soon, her breathing improved enough to come off the ventilator. Everyone's unspoken fear was that she would remain in a coma, and if she didn't, how much brain damage would she have sustained? We could only hold our breaths and hope for the best.

Several days later, Patricia bolted up singing to the praise music playing in the background! She moved all four extremities, swallowed water, talked, walked, and acted completely normal! We doctors scratched our heads. How did she sustain such a massive brain hemorrhage and come out unscathed? Why had the blasts disappeared with no treatment? It made no sense.

It made no sense, that is, until Patricia shared her near death experience with me. Patricia told me that while she was comatose, Jesus appeared to her in a translucent white robe and told her He had heard her prayers and would heal her long enough to see her daughter graduate from high school.

I stared at her in disbelief, barely able to breathe. God had granted her a miracle!

Just as promised, for the next three years, Patricia suffered no serious infections or bleeds, and her blood remained leukemia-free. She cheered for Julie at soccer games, helped her select a luscious fuchsia prom dress, and snapped untold pictures of Julie in her graduation cap and gown. Julie headed off to college to begin a four-year nursing program.

Within three months of Julie starting college, Patricia's leukemia returned with a vengeance, and this time nothing stopped it. Sadly, Patricia died of an overwhelming fungal infection shortly after receiving a bone marrow transplant donated from a stranger whose bone marrow matched hers.

Why didn't God heal Patricia permanently? Was it because we had only prayed for her to live long enough to see her daughter graduate?

Julie, not surprisingly, went on to become an oncology nurse. While sad about her mother's untimely death, she still marvels at how God allowed her mother to survive a massive brain and lung hemorrhage so she could glean her love and guidance an additional three years. Julie carries pictures in her wallet of her mother styling her hair for the homecoming dance, and standing in front of Old Faithful, and riding a mule to the bottom of the Grand Canyon. "We both knew she was here on borrowed time. Those extra three years with Mom meant everything to me because they were a gift from God. I know where Mom is, and someday, I'll be with her again."

"He performs wonders that cannot be fathomed,
miracles that cannot be counted."

~ JOB 9:10 (NIV)

Not a Single Plate Fell

Like most grandparents, Mr. and Mrs. Sutton adored caring for their three grandchildren. But one day, when a powerful tornado twisted its way straight toward their home in Murfreesboro, Tennessee, the local television weatherman admonished everyone to seek cover immediately. They piled into the downstairs master-bedroom closet along with their three grandchildren, two large dogs, and a cat! The children, shaking and terrified, clung to their grandparents and tried not to cry. As the sound of the funnel cloud swirled closer, Mr. Sutton led the family in prayer, begging God to protect them.

Soon, the dreaded "freight train" ripped through with a deafening roar. They clutched onto each other, hearts pounding. They held their breath, unwilling to voice their fear: Would they all be killed?

When everything quieted down, Mr. Sutton crept out of the closet and discovered a horrifying but miraculous sight. Their entire house had been decimated. Demolished. Even five massive oak trees in the back yard lay uprooted in the yard, except for the one that had clobbered the entire front half of their house. The kitchen, den, living room, and bedroom were history. In fact, the *only* place *not* destroyed was the very closet where the family had huddled together and prayed. Even more amazing, on the only standing bedroom wall hung a collection of decorative plates. *Not a single plate fell!*

Christians call this divine intervention. Agnostics dismiss it as sheer coincidence. Me? I say their guardian angel deserves a raise!

"The angel of the Lord encamps around those who fear Him, and He delivers them."

~ PSALMS 34:7 (NIV)

"Seize the moment. Remember all those women on the Titanic who waved off the dessert tray."

~ ERMA BOMBACK

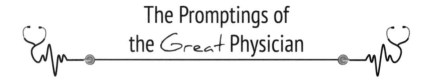

The Promptings of the Great Physician

Sometimes God's miracles involve infusing physicians with a wisdom or insight they would not otherwise have on their own. Theologians call this the "Gift of Knowledge." Like most Christian doctors, I frequently pray for my patients and for God to assist me in making a proper diagnosis, especially when a case is unclear.

I'll never forget the day a beautiful twenty-four-year-old came into the office claiming she wanted a preventive health visit. She was slim, didn't smoke or drink, ate healthy, wore sun block and a seat belt, never texted while driving, and exercised regularly. Thus, I didn't have much to advise! She'd already had her annual Pap smear with her gynecologist. More puzzling, she had no job or health insurance, and in my experience, unemployed patients without insurance usually don't come to the doctor unless they're half dead. So something deeper must have prompted her visit—but what? Her physical exam was entirely normal, and she volunteered no problems on her Review of Systems form. I prayed and asked God to help me uncover whatever she was hiding. Suddenly, an inaudible voice said to me, "This girl has bulimia."

My heart lurched in my chest. Of course, but what now? If I told her, "God just told me you're bulimic," and she wasn't, I'd look crazy—psychotic, even.

I plunged forward, as a confidence and peace that God had given me this insight to help her emboldened me. "A lot of girls your age struggle to stay slim by self-inducing vomiting. Has that ever been a temptation for you?"

The girl's eyes bulged, and she burst into tears. She had started the practice back in high school. Initially, it was only if she'd binged, but soon, it became nearly every meal. Now it consumed her life—three and four times a day, thousands of calories, every day. Now unemployed, she could no longer afford all the wasted food! She knew she needed help, but had been too ashamed to tell anyone.

I listened to her full story, prescribed fluoxetine—shown to help bulimics—and supplied the phone number of a local eating disorder twelve-step group, since she couldn't afford a counselor. We arranged a follow-up appointment for three weeks.

Once her secret was confessed, and she received proper treatment and support, she did well. I'm so grateful God gave me this word of knowledge, as truthfully, bulimia hadn't crossed my mind; I'd seen no obvious stigmata on her physical exam to clinch the diagnosis. He truly is the Great Physician.

"If any of you lacks wisdom, ask God,
who gives generously to all without finding fault,
and it will be given to you."

~ JAMES 1:5 (NIV)

To Know or *Not* to Know

At age thirty, Carol had a monumental decision to make. Her mother had a neurological disease called Huntington's chorea, and thus, genetically, Carol had a 50 percent risk of developing the dreadful disease herself. If she had inherited her father's gene, however, she'd remain neurologically normal and could not transmit the disease to any future children. Neurological Russian roulette, if you will.

Unfortunately, victims show no signs of the disease until they are in their forties or fifties, past the age of child bearing. Thus, they have already passed on the gene to half their children before they even knew they had the disease.

Carol witnessed her mother and grandmother's progressive insanity and the involuntary flailing motions of their arms and legs called chorea. Both women died of the disease around age sixty, so Carol knew only too well what torment Huntington's chorea hurled, not only to the women she loved, but to their families.

For years, Carol was burdened with not knowing whether she'd inherited the Huntington's gene or not. Plus, her whole identity had been defined and scarred by the disease. As a teen, she was so ashamed of her mother's verbal outbursts and facial grimaces, she never dared to invite a friend to her house. In her twenties, when most women dated and chose a mate, Carol refused to allow herself to get close to anyone. How could she burden a man she loved with an insane woman doomed to die early? How could she give him children if they might inherit the curse known as Huntington's chorea?

The one time she had allowed herself to fall in love and trust a man enough to bring him home, the man bolted after meeting her mother and realizing this could be his wife in the future if he were to marry Carol. Plus, children were out of the question.

Thus, Carol limped through life alone, ashamed, and afraid to reveal her deep, dark secret. Marriage and children—the deepest longing of her heart—remained locked up like Rapunzel in an ivory tower.

In the 1990s, tests were developed that could pick up the Huntington's gene even in those not yet showing signs of the disease. Instead of waiting until symptoms of the disease either did or did not manifest themselves, children and young adults could now find out early if they were doomed or free of the dread disease.

The new test could open a Pandora's Box: did she *want* to know? What if, at age thirty, she now knew with certainty she was doomed to insanity and years of neurological decline? What would living with such a dire prognosis do to her current life? Was she better off living with the glimmer of hope that she might be spared?

Meaty questions, these.

I performed a Med-line computer search to see if those who had already chosen to be tested were glad they had after receiving their results. Obviously, those who discovered they and their future children were 100 percent disease-free were elated. But what about those who discovered they were doomed to suffer and die with such a horrific disease? Did they run out and shoot themselves? Fall into a severe depression? Live in denial? Turn to drugs and drink to numb the pain?

The results surprised me: While a tiny minority did respond with suicide or drugs, the vast majority were *glad* to know the truth so they could move on with their lives. Many tackled items on their bucket lists—travel and hobbies—and chose to make the best of the time they had left. Yes, they were forced to give up any thought of birthing children, but most felt it gave them time to prepare for their future and to make the best of the time they had left.

I shared my results with Carol, and she wrestled with the

daunting decision. To know or not to know, that was the question. In the end, Carol chose genetic testing. "I've lived my whole life as though I already have the gene. I won't allow myself to get close to anyone. If I found out I didn't have the gene, I could live without fear and dread. I could even get married and have children."

I swabbed the inside of Carol's cheek and mailed off the specimen for genetic testing. She then endured an interminable two-week wait for the test results.

What if she'd made the wrong decision? What if she couldn't handle the bad news and killed herself? I could only pray we'd made the right decision to test her.

Two weeks later when the results arrived, I called her back into my office. She gripped her chair, eyes wide and radiating abject terror.

I smiled. "Carol, you don't have the gene. You're free! You're free to marry. Free to have children. Free to go about your life like everyone else."

Her shoulders heaved, and she sobbed, too overcome to speak. Her worst nightmare was finally over.

She wiped her eyes and when able to speak said, "You have no idea what a gift you've given me. For the first time ever, I can finally have a life!" She squeezed my hands in gratitude, as though I were a genie who had just granted her wish.

I gave her a big hug, delighted she could now live a life free from fear and dread and shame.

Here's the question of the day: would you want to know?

"I think we consider too much the good luck of the early bird and not enough the bad luck of the early worm."

~ FRANKLIN D. ROOSEVELT

How Her Cancer
Saved His Life

Darcie and Dean Mullins met in high school and soon became soul mates. After she completed her nursing degree, they married, and then, over the next decade, birthed four girls.

Life was good until the unthinkable happened. While tying a scarf around her neck, Darcie felt a hard lump. When it didn't recede over the next month, she consulted me because as an RN, Darcie worried it might be lymphoma.

When her lymph node excision did indeed confirm lymphoma, Darcie was devastated. How would her family survive without her?

She and Dean resolved to fight and win.

After three rounds of chemotherapy, Darcie's long, beautiful hair began to fall out in droves. Soon, only irregular clumps stuck out from her scalp, like a mutilated wig. Even a ball cap couldn't disguise her massive hair loss.

Darcie brushed away her tears and made an appointment to have her head shaved. She'd have to resort to a wig.

While not a vain woman, Darcie's luxurious black tresses had always ranked as her one crowning beauty. The thought of baldness and wigs sunk her into an emotional abyss. Would a bald wife repulse her husband? Would she ever feel healthy again? Would she even survive?

An hour before the salon appointment, Dean discovered Darcie sobbing inconsolably. He'd never seen her so broken. "Look at me! I'm so ugly," she cried. "How can you possibly find me attractive when I look like a circus freak?"

He pulled her into his arms and tried to reassure her, but he felt powerless. Other than prayer and taking over the housework, what more could he do to show his support? Then it dawned on him: he'd keep his head shaved as long as she was bald.

Since he, too, had always been blessed with a head full of thick hair, he understood her feelings of loss as he watched his curly locks hit the floor. *I just won't look at myself in the mirror.*

"I have a suspicious looking mole on my shoulder."

When he jumped up from the salon chair to pay the bill, his wife's eyes bulged in horror. She fingered his scalp and said, "How long has this mole been on your scalp?"

Since he'd always had a head full of hair, he had no idea. Given its irregular border and ominous black color, Darcie knew enough to be worried. She scheduled him an appointment with a dermatologist.

Just as she feared, the biopsy confirmed melanoma. Luckily, it was caught in the nick of time. They marveled at the timing.

Had Darcie not developed lymphoma, Dean would never have shaved his head. Had Dean not shaved his head in support of his wife, the melanoma would not have been discovered until it was too late.

I'm happy to report both Darcie and Dean are alive and well eight years after their harrowing double dose of cancer. Darcie likes to tease, "My lymphoma saved his life."

"Carry out a random act of kindness with no expectation of reward, safe in the knowledge that one day someone might do the same for you."

~ PRINCESS DIANA

In the Blink of an Eye ...

In the blink of an eye, a robust college student is struck by a bolt of lightning, goes into a prolonged cardiac arrest, and ends up in a vegetative state. Fifteen years later, he's still comatose.

In the blink of an eye, a cauliflower-like growth on a young man's heart valve travels from his heart to his brain, triggering a massive embolic stroke. He'll never walk or speak clearly again.

In the blink of an eye, a train pummels the car of a talented and well-liked cheerleader. She is killed on impact.

In the blink of an eye, a favorite aunt of mine is killed in a freak accident caused by a drunk driver.

Why ... ?

We all love stories of miracles and answered prayers, while stories about teens left comatose and the senseless death of people we love challenge our faith. Why didn't God intervene and prevent such tragedies?

Some tragedies we can blame on poor choices: drinking and driving, drug abuse, not wearing seat belts, or not seeking shelter during a lightning storm. We console ourselves that we would never be so stupid, and our sense of control is restored.

Yet, a patient of mine, a much-loved wife and mother, died of ovarian cancer through no fault of her own. Why her and not me? Why must *her* two little girls be left without a mother, while my children are blessed with two loving parents? What about a young patient of mine who was brutally gang raped?

Truthfully, I hate these cases. They anger me and make me ask, "How could a loving God stand by and do nothing? Why did He miraculously heal my patient with leukemia, but not the mother with ovarian cancer? Free will comes with a price,

I'm told, but what about the free will of the raped teenager? The free will of children left with no mother? Bad events often seem arbitrary and unfair.

Why couldn't the "nice" people be spared, while the evildoers get what's coming to them? Unfortunately, life doesn't work that way. Scripture says God loves us all and that the sun and rain fall on the good *and* evil alike.

As a physician, I've had to grapple with countless tragedies in the lives of my patients. My faith can be rattled when God doesn't run this planet the way I think He should. Why doesn't He rescue and heal people more if He's so all-powerful? How can He sit on His throne doing nothing when His children are facing calamity, especially if the calamity is not their fault, or young children are involved? Troublesome questions, these.

God doesn't fit into a tidy little box; He's not a genie in a jar offering to grant me three wishes. He never has, and He never will be.

James 5:16 says: "The prayer of a righteous man availeth much." I have personally witnessed miracles and answered prayers, but why don't all my prayers "availeth much?" In short, sometimes God makes no sense, and my faith is occasionally weakened.

It all boils down to this: *Do I trust you, God? Even when I don't understand why, when things aren't fair? Even when the outcome suggests You aren't listening and don't care?*

After years of struggling with this thorny issue and an exhaustive study of books on the subject, my answer is yes. I can either chose to see humans as powerless pawns on a cruel chessboard, or I can choose to believe God is in control and somehow has what's best for us in mind. When I see God's power in lightning or a tornado, or His attention to beauty and detail in a gorgeous sunset or flower, I know He is not incapable. He must have a higher purpose I don't understand.

Romans 8:28 says God can use even the worst tragedy for

good *if* we choose to surrender everything to Him and let Him use our circumstances—no matter how tragic— for some benefit we may never know in our earthly lifetime. As humans, we don't have the perspective of heaven or eternity. Scripture says our lives are but a puff of smoke compared to all eternity. That is the perspective that I, as a human physician, don't have. However, He is beyond time and space. He is the Great Physician, and as a result, He has eternal perspective. Thus, I don't have to understand Him to trust Him.

Do I trust You, God? Most of the time I do. Please help me when I don't.

"O, the depth of the riches and the wisdom and knowledge of God! How unsearchable are his judgments! How inscrutable are his ways!"

~ ROMANS 11:13 (ENGLISH STANDARD)

Patients
Who Made
Me Laugh

Bad, Bad Leroy Brown

Worry lines creased Marsha's forehead. "I swear, my father won't die of Alzheimer's—I'm going to kill him first!"

Sensing she needed to vent about the challenges of caring for her demented father, I invited Marsha to clue me in.

At ninety-four, Leroy Brown—name changed to protect the guilty—had trash and junk piled to the ceiling of his Detroit home. The only food in the refrigerator was beer and moldy pizza. He hadn't taken his blood pressure pill in months, and the electric department had turned off his power for nonpayment. He'd recently gotten confused driving home from the grocery store and ended up two counties away and out of gas. In short, his Alzheimer's disease had progressed to the point where he could no longer care for himself. Marsha flew to Detroit and located a competent nurse's aide to cook, clean, pay bills, and keep an eye on him.

Two days later, however, the aide called to resign. Why? Every time she attempted to show up for

"Darling, I wish you'd stop the self defense classes, now you've got Alzheimer's."

work, Leroy brandished a rifle at her and hollered, "Get your fat a** off my property, or I'll shoot!" Marsha flew back to Detroit, seized the rifle, and came up with plan B. This time, she dug up a caregiver who agreed to move into the house in exchange for free rent and food. Marsha helped her settle into the guest bedroom. "Don't you worry," she insisted, patting Marsha's hand. "I've dealt with plenty of Alzheimer's patients before."

Three weeks later, the caregiver called and was moving out—today! The old geezer had exposed himself on multiple occasions, and now was groping at her and insisting if she was going to live in his house, she had better earn her keep—and he didn't mean by cleaning the toilet!

Marsha flew back to Detroit for a third time. She moved him into an assisted-living program against his will. A week later, she received a frantic call from the facility. "Leroy crawled out of his second story window, using his sheet as a rope. We have no idea where he is." Since it was nighttime in the dead of winter, the police were called to help locate him before he froze to death. Eight hours later, they found him all right—warm and toasty—watching television in his recliner back at his house! Even though the assisted-living facility was four miles away, he had apparently walked in his bathrobe and slippers until "some guy in a truck" offered him a ride. He made no apology for the angst he'd caused. "It's your own &%$# fault. I told you I didn't want to live in that old folks' home."

Fed up with his tomfoolery, Marsha admitted him to a nursing home that locked its front door and had no windows from which to crawl out. Before the day was over, nurses scolded him for profane language, pinching and groping, and flinging Brussels sprouts at a chatty resident in the dining room who grated on his nerves. One day, he stuffed a sock in the mouth of a fellow Alzheimer's patient. "It's her own *&%# fault. I told her to shut up, but she wouldn't stop hollering."

Then the unthinkable happened. Late one night, another

nursing home resident, Mr. Williams, became confused and shuffled with his walker into Leroy's room by mistake. Startled by the "prowler," Leroy picked up his cane and began clobbering the poor man. The nurse on duty heard the commotion and ran into the room just in time to witness Mr. Williams thrusting his walker—legs first—toward Leroy, as though it were a shield. Leroy struck back with his cane, as though it were a sword. Before the nurse could stop him, Leroy administered such a hard whack both men landed on the floor in a heap. Security broke up the brawl, and Mr. Williams was ambulanced to the hospital for X-rays. Leroy managed to escape unscathed, but he refused to apologize. Arms crossed, he snapped, "It was his fault. He shouldn't have been prowling in my room. I thought he was a burglar."

After Leroy's latest antics, thoughts of patricide entered Marsha's head. What was she going to do with the incorrigible old cuss?

Because of the brawl, Leroy was kicked out of the nursing home and admitted to the psychiatric ward for evaluation. As though sensing he was doomed for powerful psych drugs or electric shock therapy if he didn't behave himself, Leroy suddenly became a model patient: pleasant, clean-mouthed, and he even managed to keep his hands to himself. When Marsha walked in, he had the nurses and doctors in stitches at his humorous tales from World War II. He had hoodwinked them all. The psychiatrist remarked, "Leroy was just defending himself from whom he thought was a prowler. He's acting out because he needs more activity and stimulation."

Leroy heartily agreed as he ogled the attractive nurse nearby. He then turned to Marsha. "I *told* you nothing was wrong with me. *You're* the one with the problem."

The problem was hers all right—what to do with Leroy! If he didn't straighten up soon, *she* would land in the psych ward with a mental breakdown. Or jail, for murder.

The nursing home refused to take him back. After begging and pleading, she cajoled another nursing home into admitting him. At the advice of the psychiatrist, he was enrolled in mentally and physically stimulating activities, such as arts and crafts, shuffleboard, and physical therapy. Unfortunately, he was banned from arts and crafts after offending the lady participants with his vulgar crayon drawings of voluptuous nude women. He was banned from shuffleboard after he lost a game and flung his cue and broke it in a fit of rage. The stick had missed another resident's head by mere inches. Maybe physical therapy was the ticket . . .

The physical therapist enrolled Leroy in a program using elastic bands and five-pound weights. Since Leroy also suffered from arthritis in his knees, the therapist focused on strengthening his quadriceps.

One day, Leroy wasn't in the mood for therapy and refused to participate.

"Come on, Leroy, it'll be good for you," the therapist insisted.

"I don't want to." He pursed his lips and crossed his arms like a petulant child.

"Oh silly me, I'm trying to fix my glasses with nasal spray instead of super glue!"

"You can do it," the therapist encouraged. "I insist you at least give it a try." He pulled Leroy off the bed and into a standing position. "It'll strengthen your knees."

Annoyed that the therapist hadn't listened to him, Leroy walloped his bent knee straight into the crotch of the therapist.

The therapist howled and doubled over in pain as Leroy said, "Nothing wrong with that knee. Want me to show you how well the other knee works, too?"

The therapist limped from the room and refused to EVER work on Leroy again. Of course, Marsha was called yet again. "What can I do?" she snapped at the head of the nursing home. "I'm here in Nashville, and I can't afford to miss any more work. He is costing me a fortune. Deal with it." She slammed down the phone, frustrated beyond measure.

Leroy was sent back to the psych ward, but this time they prescribed potent medications to keep him calm. While she hated the thought of him doped up, at least no more people ended up in the ER—or sterilized. Once sedated, he was sent back to the nursing home, this time compliant.

"Not only is my short-term memory horrible, but so is my short-term memory."

~ BILL MURRAY

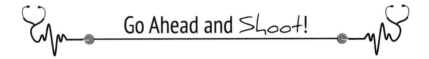

Go Ahead and Shoot!

By age ninety, Lillian Orson was one tough old bird. She'd survived near starvation in the Great Depression, the loss of two brothers in World War II, a devastating house fire, and the recent death of her husband. Thus, when approached by a thief in the parking garage of the local mall, Lillian was not about to hand over her purse without a fight.

The thief pointed his gun at her and hissed, "Give me your purse, or I'll shoot."

She clutched her purse to her chest and snapped, "Go ahead and shoot! I'm ninety years old, and I've lived a good life. I'm ready to meet my Maker. What about you? You want to face the Almighty after robbing an old lady living on nothing more than a Social Security check?"

She jabbed a finger in his chest. "You should be ashamed of yourself, young man! Besides, I've only got ten dollars in here. You want to land in prison over ten bucks?"

The robber, not expecting such a feisty old broad, bolted!

> *"Cowards die many times before their deaths; the valiant never taste of death but once."*
>
> ~ **WILLIAM SHAKESPEARE**

The Fat Old Lady and the Water Bucket

When American medical suppliers outsourced jobs to China, we not only lost millions of jobs, we doomed patients to embarrassing physical exams. Huh? Let me explain:

In China, where an average woman is lucky to reach five feet tall and weigh one hundred pounds, a "large" patient is anyone over five foot four who weighs one hundred twenty pounds. Not so in America, where the average woman tips the scale at one hundred sixty pounds and is lucky to cram her hefty hips into size fourteen jeans. Therein lies the problem—skinny, short Asians produce the paper patient gowns that obese American women are supposed to don for their annual exams. Thus, an appropriate "extra-large" gown for the Chinese will only fit the most anorectic of Americans. My patients all grumble about my scanty paper gowns, and some have accused me of turning them into streakers when they dash across the hall to provide a urine sample. Here's the rub—no American manufacturer produces affordable paper gowns.

Never was this issue more glaring than the day Mrs. Bryce came in for her yearly evaluation. Mrs. Bryce, a jolly senior citizen who tipped the scale at three hundred pounds, sat perched on the exam table waiting for me to enter the room and complete her exam.

Unfortunately, my extra-large gown barely covered her bottom, let alone the pendulous breasts hanging clear to her waist. Since my exam rooms on the sixth floor have large picture windows, she was enjoying the view of Krispy Kreme when suddenly, a thick rope with a bucket of water appeared in the picture window right in front of her. It didn't take a Rhodes scholar to figure out a window-washer would be next.

When I entered the room, Mrs. Bryce told me about the sudden appearance of the rope and bucket. "You've never seen a fat old lady move so fast in your life." Despite her arthritic knees and obesity, she hopped down and closed the blinds before the window washer obtained "the peep show from hell," as she called it.

Since obesity rates continue to climb, perhaps I could get rich quick by investing in an American manufacturing plant that produces paper gowns in the following sizes: Roly-poly, Jumbo, Humongous, and for the morbidly corpulent, Elephantine.

"It's time to go on a diet when you've got more rolls than a pastry shop."

~ AUTHOR UNKNOWN

The Funeral Parlor Director's
Embarrassing Day

The obese patient about to expose herself to the window washer may have been embarrassed, but not as much as a certain funeral parlor director. James Montgomery owned the largest funeral parlor in the county. A respected business leader and deacon in the church, he strove to keep his reputation spotless.

But a lifetime of brittle diabetes had taken its toll, and James had developed impotency to such a degree that even Viagra proved, well, impotent. His urologist suggested an inflatable implant that could be pumped up immediately before relations with his wife, thereby allowing him to continue the intimacy they'd enjoyed for decades.

James consented to the procedure and while he was still groggy from anesthesia, his nurse demonstrated how to inflate the implant. Finally, he could reclaim his manhood.

Once the incision was fully healed, he was eager to try out the new device. He surprised his wife by taking an early lunch hour one day, where he presented her with flowers and silky, new lingerie. Delighted with the romantic gesture, she moseyed into the bedroom. James was quick to follow. He inflated the implant exactly as the nurse had instructed him, and the couple enjoyed their first consummated relations in over two years.

Ready to return to work, James realized with sudden horror that he couldn't remember exactly how to *deflate* his now fully erect penis. Had the nurse even taught him? He scoured the hospital discharge papers for instructions. No luck. Worse still, the urologist's office was closed for another hour for their lunch break.

What was he going to do? He had a funeral to officiate at 1:30 p.m., and the implant made his anatomy protrude in an inappropriate way. He'd look like a pervert! People might think he got his jollies from dead people!

Clients were depending on him, so James officiated the funeral, trying his best to keep his privates covered by holding the deceased's bulletin in front of him at all times. He thought he'd escaped detection until his co-worker, who knew about the recent implant, whispered to him, "Don't they have a release valve on that thing?"

James wanted to crawl into the nearest coffin and slam the lid. Ego deflated, he cloistered himself in his office until the urologist's office reopened, and he could rectify the situation.

"Nothing is as embarrassing as watching your boss do something you assured him could not be done."

~ EARL WILSON

Mama Sure Looked *Nice*

Speaking of funeral parlors, one patient had an encounter with a dead body in an entirely different way. It upset her so much, she scheduled an appointment with me to discuss it. She gripped the arms of her chair, stress etched across her forehead. "I either need a new job or a bottle of Valium," she'd insisted. She worked in customer service at an expensive department store in town. *How could that be so difficult?*

She then told me about a customer she'd dealt with this week: The woman had purchased an exquisite dress several days earlier for her mother's funeral. Now that the funeral was over, she wanted to return the dress and get her money back even though the dress emitted a peculiar, pungent odor.

Turns out, the woman had purchased the dress not for herself, *but for her dead mother*! She wanted her mother to look elegant in her casket for the calling hours and funeral! Once the funeral was over, however, the daughter had removed the expensive dress from her mother's corpse immediately before the lid of the coffin was shut and her mother lowered into the cemetery plot. She now insisted on returning the dress and getting a full refund! Never mind it reeked of embalming fluids. Never mind a dead person wore it for hours in a coffin.

When my patient refused to take the dress back, the customer pitched a hissy fit. "Why not? Mama was dead, and a dead person can't hurt that dress none."

My patient held her ground, and the customer stormed out in a huff. "If I'd known you wouldn't take it back, I'd have buried her in it."

Gone to the Dogs

Speaking of challenges, one of the greatest struggles for doctors is obtaining a competent answering service for night and weekend phone coverage. Too frequently, the operators bungle up which doctor is on call, or they provide an inaccurate phone number. Sometimes, they just don't answer the phone. I once had a patient tell me she let the phone ring forty-five times—she actually counted the rings—before the answering service employee bothered to pick up the receiver.

The worst experience I endured was after midnight on New Year's Eve when I was on call for six doctors. The answering service paged me and claimed they had an urgent call. Sure enough, I was greeted by a frantic male voice: "Brandy keeps having accidents. There's poop everywhere. You've got to do something."

"Her stools are so runny she can't make it to the toilet, you mean?" I inquired.

I heard a snicker. "Naw, she goes outside."

Outside? Did people still use outhouses? Boy, was this guy backwoods!

"So you don't have an indoor toilet for Brandy to use?"

A long pause. "Doc, I ain't never heard of a dog using a toilet before. Is that something new they're teaching in obedience classes these days?"

I nearly dropped the phone. *Dog obedience classes??* "BRAN-

DY'S A DOG??"

"Yes. Brandy's my cocker spaniel. Aren't you Dr. Eubanks, Brandy's veterinarian?

"No, I'm a medical doctor. I treat people." I explained the mix-up, and we both had a good laugh. No doubt about it. Our answering service had "gone to the dogs."

Answering Service: "How can I help you?"

Patient: "Dr. Burbank diagnosed me with pneumonia yesterday, but I have a friend whose doctor told him he had pneumonia and he just died of tuberculosis. I'm worried."

Answering Service: "Don't worry! If Dr. Burbank said you've got pneumonia, you'll die of pneumonia!"

Menopause: Give Me Hormones, or Give Me Death

A husband accompanying his wife to her doctor's appointment is always a bad sign. It typically signifies fear of cancer, a broken foot, hearing voices, fainting, chest pain, or something equally as ominous.

Thus, when I noted Patrick Morrison sitting in my exam room next to his wife, I braced myself.

Imagine my shock when the first words out of his mouth were, "Doctor Burbank, you HAVE to give my wife hormones. It's that, or I'm calling a divorce attorney, and the kids are calling the Department of Children's Services."

"I'm not that bad," she hissed in a tone that could curdle honey. Since I knew Patrick and his wife, Sandra, had been happily married for nearly two decades, I asked them to clue me in.

Arms folded defiantly across her chest, Sandra snapped, "Menopause should be outlawed."

For starters, Sandra kept the air conditioning cranked so high, the rest of the family had resorted to wearing winter coats. "You can pile on more clothes, but I can't walk around the house naked," she retorted when one of them had dared to complain about how cold the house was.

Sandra chewed her husband's head off for the slightest infraction, like leaving his socks on the bathroom floor, not loading the dishwasher to her liking, and my favorite, forgetting to dust the clock radio in their bedroom. Sandra would then burst into tears, sob, and lament what a terrible wife she was for screaming at him like that. Why didn't he just leave her because she was a h-horrible p-person, sob, sob, sob, and w-why did he p-put up with her? He could have done so much b-better, and she was so f-fat, ugly, and irritable, sob, sob, sob, and he had every right to w-w-walk out on her. All over a clock radio that hadn't been dusted!

Patrick, also a patient of mine, had played the role of long-suffering husband for five months now. He knew she was menopausal, and with the 2006 study showing a slight increase in breast cancer and leg clot risk among women who took hormonal replacement therapy, he had discouraged her from taking estrogen.

"So what's changed your mind?" I inquired. "Why are you willing to incur these risks now?"

The two looked at each other. Dead silence. Then Sandra looked away, picking at a hangnail. "You tell her."

Patrick filled me in: One night at the dinner table, Sandra got one of her horrific hot flashes. "The hot flash from hell," she insisted.

Her two sons, aged thirteen and sixteen, were sitting at the dinner table munching on fried chicken when suddenly, they saw their mother flushed and perspiring. Next thing they knew, she had flung off her blouse and was sitting at the table clad only in her bra from the waist up.

Her two boys, eyes now the size of moon pies, said, "Mom! What are you doing?"

Sandra, now fanning herself frantically with the bread plate, glared at them. "You don't know what a hot flash is like!"

The younger snapped, "And I don't want to, if this is how they make you behave!"

The two boys glanced across the table at their father, hoping he'd do something about her troubling behavior. Instead, his eyebrows knit together with the unspoken message: *Ignore her*. He gestured with his head toward their dinner plates, and he began munching on his biscuit, as though a fifty-year-old woman sitting at the dinner table wearing only a bra from the waist up in front of her two teenaged sons looking horrified was perfectly normal. Patrick, trying not to trigger one of her verbal tirades or crying jags in front of the boys, kept his mouth shut and focused on buttering his biscuit.

Following their father's lead, the boys completed their dinner as though nothing were amiss. After the meal, however, the oldest took his father aside. "Dad, you've got to do something about Mom. She's completely out of control. Yesterday, she screamed at my girlfriend for leaving a Coke can on the end table instead of putting it in the recycling dumpster. Then she started bawling her eyes out, and she ran out of the room saying she was a terrible mother. I was so embarrassed, and now Danielle refuses to come to the house."

Hence, the visit to my office. Patrick beseeched me to prescribe his wife hormones—in high doses.

After a long discussion with them both about the risks and benefits, we opted for a one or two-year course of HRT. We'd try to taper off in a year.

"It's that or the loony bin," Sandra said with a hint of a smile. "Besides, with two sons to fund through college, divorce is out of the question!"

He smiled. "We'll get through this menopause thing together, just like every other crisis we've faced."

Thankfully, with the addition of hormones, Sandra was soon back to the loving wife and mother she used to be.

Menopause is definitely not for sissies!

"The seven dwarves of menopause: Itchy, Witchy, Sweaty, Sleepy, Bloated, Forgetful, and Psycho."

~ Author Unknown

Honesty:
An Overrated
Virtue

Miss Ruby's Rebuke

I had just completed an annual physical on Miss Ruby, a feisty eighty-year-old retired nurse, when she turned to me and snapped, "Dr. Sally, why have you let yourself get so fat? If I had let myself go like that, you'd be jumping all over me. You need to lose some weight!"

Ouch! I wanted to slither into the red plastic sharps container located in the corner of the exam room, if only my lardy legs, blubbery belly, and chubby chins would fit. Pokes from contaminated needles beat the humiliation of her scolding eyes.

Must she be so blunt? Even fat female physicians have feelings. And talk about role reversal—she, the patient, was telling me, the physician, to lose weight? Awkward.

Yes, I admit it. I've put on twenty-five pounds in the last fifteen years, and it isn't pretty. So hang me from a pole—preferably one where the rope is made from link sausages and string cheese—but not until after my Saturday lunch date at the Puffy Muffin. I need Weight Watchers. And Jenny Craig. And a whole lot less French Silk ice cream. What I didn't need was some whipper-snapper point-

"Relax. I'm the <u>Trim</u> Reaper. I'm here for her flabby thighs and your spare tire."

CartoonStock.com

ing it out. Does she think the mirror doesn't scold me for the weight gain every time I dare to look?

Unfortunately, Miss Ruby wasn't the only one to singe my ego. A month ago, another patient inquired, "When is the baby due?" I bit my tongue from snapping back, "Look sister, you're no Skinny Minnie yourself!" I didn't know whether to cry because she thought I looked fat enough to be pregnant, or jump for joy that, at age fifty-four, she thought I still looked young enough to get pregnant.

My mortifying encounter with Miss Ruby was unfortunately not over. As she exited the exam room, she wagged a finger in my face. "I'll expect to see a lot *less* of you at my three-month follow-up."

Honesty, I've decided, is an overrated virtue!

"I'm not offended by all the dumb blonde jokes because I know I'm not dumb. I also know I'm not blonde."

~ DOLLY PARTON

Still Alive? Prove It!

Speaking of honesty, the Social Security Administration must face an oversupply of shysters hoping to bilk the system, because they view most appeals for money with jaded eyes. In the case of one of my patients, their hypervigilance nearly starved her to death.

Eighty-five-year-old Marian Beckham's husband had passed away two months earlier. A homemaker, she was entitled to half of her late husband's Social Security benefits. She was too grief-stricken the first month after his death to notice she hadn't received her usual check. After the second month with no check, however, she became concerned and called the Social Security Administration. After weaving through an intimidating web of voice mail options, she finally reached a live human being.

The employee researched the complaint and then informed her, "You haven't received a check because, according to our computer, you're dead. You died two months ago."

Brow furrowed, Marian said, "My *husband* died two months ago, but I'm very much alive, and I need that check."

"Unless you can prove you're alive, we can't reinstate your Social Security check," the unsympathetic clerk informed her.

"Prove I'm alive? I'm talking on the phone with you, and I'm not calling from heaven." Marian clenched the phone, disgusted with the runaround. "Doesn't *that* prove I'm alive? We obviously have a computer error."

"Or an imposter trying to steal Marian Beckham's identity so she can swindle checks out of the Social Security Administration. We see it all the time," the clerk said.

Dumbfounded, my patient ended the call and decided to

drive to the Social Security Administration to resolve the matter. Surely if she showed up in person with a driver's license and birth certificate, they'd resume her check.

No such luck. After waiting in line until her knees needed replacing, she slapped down her documents on the desk of the cynical clerk. The clerk barely glanced at them before shoving them back. "This doesn't prove a thing. You could have stolen these."

Marian jabbed her finger on the driver's license. "That's my name and my picture. An imposter wouldn't look like me."

The clerk shrugged. "How do I know you're not Marian's identical twin trying to steal her identity and swindle the system?"

Marian scowled. "*Because I don't have an identical twin.* I don't even have a sister." Nerves frayed, Marian snapped, "What's wrong with you people? Obviously, my name was inadvertently changed to dead when my husband passed away two months ago. We're dealing with a computer glitch, plain and simple, and I want it fixed," she said, arms crossed. "I need that check; my pantry is empty."

The hardened clerk cocked an eyebrow. "All I know is, our computer says Marian L. Beckham is dead, and until you can prove she *isn't* dead and that you are in fact Marian L. Beckham, I can't reinstate your Social Security checks."

Marian released a heavy sigh. "How do I prove I'm not dead if standing here in person with my birth certificate and driver's license isn't enough?"

The clerk pursed her lips. "Get your personal physician to write a certified letter testifying you are who you say you are and that you are not dead. I would consider that proof that the computer made a mistake."

That's where I came in. Marian rushed to my office, explained her frustrating encounter, and asked me to write a letter on her behalf. It is the oddest letter I have ever written:

Dear Social Security Administration,

Marian L. Beckham has been my patient for ten years. She came into my office requesting a letter stating she is not dead. Therefore, I, Sally Burbank, MD, do hereby legally testify that Marian L. Beckham is not dead, nor has she ever been dead. Please resume her Social Security checks.

Sincerely,

Sally Burbank, MD

The letter worked. Her checks were reinstated.

"The reports of my death have been greatly exaggerated."

~ MARK TWAIN

Crocks—And I Don't Mean the Shoes

Over the years, I have encountered pa-tients who, unlike Mari-an Beckham, *did* hope to swindle the Social Secu-rity system by feigning symptoms and hoping I'd recommend them for federal disability. Every physician sees his or her

"I SCHEDULED YOU FOR 4:45 P.M. BECAUSE HE TOLD ME YOU WERE THE LAST PERSON HE WANTED TO SEE."

share of these malingerers; we refer to these shysters as crocks.

Robert was a classic. When my nurse escorted him to his exam room, he jumped right up from his chair and marched down the hall with no problem whatsoever. As soon as I walked into the room, though, he clutched his back and whimpered, "Doc, I'm in pain. Terrible pain. You gotta give me something strong cause this pain's unbearable."

Motrin, Tylenol, Bengay, you-name-it conveniently didn't touch his pain. "Doc Smith always gave me OxyContin." Swell! A drug seeker. When asked why he left Doctor Smith, he mut-tered a vague excuse and avoided eye contact, which meant Doctor Smith probably dismissed Robert from his practice for abusing narcotics, not paying his bill, or general obnoxiousness and verbal abuse to the staff. Just the patient every doctor wants.

When I asked Robert to climb up onto the exam table, you'd have thought I'd asked him to run the Boston Marathon—twice. He groaned, whined, whimpered, hollered, and stiffened his spine as though I'd stabbed a knife in his back. Even the slight-est tap on his knee with my reflex hammer elicited tortured screams and a contorted face.

Not surprisingly, he then informed me he needed help obtaining federal disability. "Obviously, I can't work with this bad back," he insisted, gripping his side and wincing in exaggerated pain.

I turned my back so he wouldn't see me roll my eyes. Perhaps I should suggest he pursue a career in theater since he enjoyed acting so much. Instead, I ordered X-rays to confirm my suspicion that nothing was wrong with his spine.

As expected, his blood work, lumbar spine X-ray, and MRI all came back normal. This left me in a quandary. If I wrote the truth on his disability form—that he was a narcotic-seeking crock hoping to bilk the system—he might sue me. But no way would I commit fraud by recommending this guy for permanent disability. Thus, I wrote the following statement: "Robert's *subjective* complaints far outweigh any *objective* findings on physical exam or MRI." This would clue the disability determination judge that Robert was a malingerer.

Not surprisingly, his appeal for disability was rejected, and within days, Robert charged into my office demanding an explanation. "Why'd you say my subjective complaints outweighed my objective findings?" He pointed at his rejection letter then glared at me. "This makes me sound like a phony."

I pasted on a shocked expression. "Robert! You totally misunderstood what I meant. I provided that statement because I wanted the judge to know how much pain you endure. After all, if he only looked at your MRI and X-ray reports, he'd think nothing was wrong with you because your objective test results were normal. I wanted the judge to know how much you suffer *despite* your normal MRI."

I could feel my nose growing an inch.

"Oh," he said, his face relaxing into a smile. "I guess I didn't read it that way the first time."

Thankfully, neither did the disability judge!

What's the Matter with Heather?

Heather was either a hypochondriac or another malingerer trying to con me into helping her obtain federal disability. Only thirty, she'd come to her doctor's appointment on a stretcher and wearing a facemask. She claimed she was too weak to walk, and the supposed "allergens and toxins" in my office would affect her immune system "for weeks." She'd recently strained her back lifting a Pepsi can.

"Just dressing myself in the morning takes hours because I'm so weak, and I hurt all over," she said.

Everything she ate caused diarrhea or made her sick, so she lived off organic rice, chicken noodle soup, and a handful of Chinese herbs and vitamins she'd purchased off the Internet.

On a checklist of one hundred possible symptoms, Heather marked yes to seventy-eight of them. Her hair was thinning, her head pounded, her thinking was cloudy, and her nails were brittle and had weird lines, and she hurt "every-

where," and her feet and hands tingled, and she felt exhausted
. . . You get the picture! And those were only seven out of her
seventy-eight complaints! At this rate, we'd be here all night!

I released a weary sigh, now exhausted myself. Heather was
such a train wreck, I barely knew where to start. So I settled on
telling her I would not fill out her disability form until I'd come
up with a definitive diagnosis for all her symptoms, and that
would require blood tests and a thorough medical evaluation.

No, that's already been done, she insisted—six times, in
fact. Her husband then handed me a pile of medical records
two feet thick generated from her last six doctors. I thumbed
through the records, but no obvious cause could be found. Four
doctors had recommended a psychiatrist, but Heather insisted
she wasn't depressed or mentally ill. Her husband insisted she
had chronic fatigue syndrome, and no more tests needed to be
done: "All you need to do is fill out the paperwork so Heather
can obtain disability checks, especially since I had to quit my
job to stay home and take care of her."

The only problem? I wasn't convinced CFS was her problem;
I had other patients with the condition, and none exhibited all
of Heather's bizarre complaints.

That night, I poured over the mountain of records in labori-
ous detail. Since Heather was penniless, I didn't want to waste
money by repeating tests that had already been done. I researched her symptoms in hopes of finding one condition that
would tie together all her complaints. Crazy as a loon came to
mind.

The other six doctors had already ruled out every condition I
could come up with *except one*: arsenic poisoning. Why on earth
would she have that? She'd never worked in a factory, wasn't a
painter, and didn't drink water from a well. Was her husband
trying to poison her? The perverse thought that I didn't blame
him entered my head.

What about those online Chinese herbs? Her husband said

she swallowed them by the fistful. The FDA doesn't test herbal products from overseas for purity or safety. *Could they be contaminated with arsenic?* Unlikely, but no harm making sure.

Sure enough, her 24-hour urine test for arsenic poisoning lit up like Las Vegas at midnight. I sent her Chinese herbs off for toxicology testing, and the report came back confirming the herbs dripped with arsenic. I was rather proud of myself for clinching the case when six other doctors hadn't.

Convinced Heather and her husband would declare "National Sally Burbank Day" in light of my brilliant discovery, I called them into the office to go over the test results and treatment options.

Instead of slathering me with praise and adoration, however, they were angry. Hostile, even! Why? Since I'd found a treatable and potentially curable condition, they would no longer qualify for long-term disability, which was their ultimate goal. For someone too weak to lift a soda can, Heather jumped off her stretcher and jabbed a finger in my chest, livid that I'd accused her precious Chinese herbs of poisoning her. "They're the only thing that's kept me alive these last two years."

They stormed out of my office, no doubt to search for another doctor willing to fill out their disability paperwork instead of treating her arsenic poisoning. I never heard from them again.

"If we doctors threw all our medicines into the sea, it would be that much better for our patients and that much worse for the fishes."

~ OLIVER WENDELL HOLMES

America's Dumbest Criminals

Ever read the *Readers' Digest* column, "America's Dumbest Criminals"? Well, three of my patients deserve stories in the column.

A woman came into my office after straining her back moving heavy furniture. Ibuprofen and Tylenol hadn't touched the pain, and her back strain kept her awake all night. I wrote a prescription for the lowest dose of a narcotic painkiller. The script read Lortab 5/325. I wrote it for 15 pills and zero refills.

Later that day, a pharmacist called me convinced the prescription had been tampered with.

"What makes you think so?" I asked.

"Because the 5/325 milligram now reads 7.5/325, the 15 pills now reads as *150* pills, and the zero refills has been altered to *ten* refills."

"What tipped you off?" I inquired.

He explained: My patient altered the script using *blue* ink even though I'd written the prescription in *black* ink. Since I keep a copy of every controlled drug prescription I write, we had definitive proof the script had been altered. The pharmacist arranged a sting

I'M SO EMBARRASSED. PLEASE DON'T TELL ANYONE I JUST FELL OFF THE TURNIP TRUCK...

ATLANTIC FEATURE © 2001 MARK PARISI   offthemark.com

operation, and she was arrested.

Another patient came to the emergency room claiming he had overdosed on his wife's Valium because he was so depressed—suicidal, even. Turned out he was scheduled to start a fifteen-year prison sentence for aggravated sexual assault the next morning. He was currently out on bail.

He waved his wife's Valium bottle at me and insisted he needed to be admitted overnight for observation and psychiatric care because of his supposed suicide attempt. When I asked how many pills he had taken, he said, "at least a dozen."

And he was still awake and talking coherently?

"How long ago did you swallow the pills?" I asked.

He averted his eyes. "A couple of hours ago, so it's too late to pump my stomach."

I didn't buy his story one bit! If he had swallowed *twelve* Valium tablets two hours ago, he should be nearly comatose, not wide-awake and conversing. Now suspicious his whole suicide attempt story was a ruse—a get-out-of-jail-free Monopoly card—I counted the pills in the bottle. His wife had filled the script two weeks earlier, and the bottle still had sixteen pills in it, suggesting he had taken none. When I confronted him, he shrugged and stared down at his feet. "She doesn't take them every day. Just when she really needs them."

Bunk! To prove my theory, I ordered a blood and urine drug screen. I also insisted on pumping out his stomach and then using charcoal slurries just in case I was wrong and he had overdosed. The emergency room doctor insisted that because he *claimed* he'd attempted suicide, we had no choice but to admit him to the hospital for observation and to obtain a psychiatric consult in the morning. We both shook our heads in disgust because we knew he was conning us to delay his prison sentence.

Just as I suspected, the drug screens came back without a trace of Valium. The idiot should have at least swallowed *one* Valium pill to validate his story and make the drug screen positive.

I wrote a letter to the court documenting his negative drug screen despite his claim of swallowing twelve pills. The judge rewarded his shenanigans with an extra year in the slammer for obstructing justice.

My third dummy patient just wanted a few extra paid days off from work, but he sure picked a stupid way to get them! He presented to my office with a severe sore throat. When his rapid strep test came back positive, I prescribed a course of penicillin and scribbled out a note for his workplace excusing him for the next two days.

Imagine my shock when the patient's boss called several days later to find out why I felt he needed TWENTY paid days off from work for a simple strep throat. Turns out, the patient had added a zero to my "2" days and made it "20" days! (At least this patient had the intelligence to use the same color ink!)

Luckily, I had kept a copy of the original work excuse, so I faxed it to the employer, and he fired his dishonest employee on the spot.

He got his twenty days off from work, all right—unemployed!

*"Some drink from the fountain for knowledge,
others merely gargle."*

~ AUTHOR UNKNOWN

Who's Got the STD?

The most egregious dishonesty involved a teenager I'll call Marcy. Ten years ago, I had identical twin college students in my practice, Marcy and Darcy. Marcy came in to see me with symptoms suggestive of a potential sexually transmitted disease, so I cultured her and told her I'd call with results. Darcy came in with her sister that day to receive her third HPV vaccine.

Several days later, Marcy's culture came back positive for gonorrhea. Despite leaving multiple subtle messages on her voice mail to call us back for some very important test results, she never responded. Since we knew the Health Department would call soon for a list of all her sexual contacts, we didn't want her to find out she had gonorrhea from an unknown Health Department STD nurse before hearing it from us. Plus, she needed treatment!

"Well you can't say that I never give you anything!"

Thus, my medical assistant decided to up the ante in her effort to get Marcy's attention, so besides mailing a certified letter, she called the cellphone number listed in Marcy's chart and left the message that she had gonorrhea and needed immediate treatment. When she left the message, however, she accidentally used the *sister's* name, *Darcy*, instead of the *patient's* name, *Marcy*.

When Marcy listened to the message on her voice mail stating that Darcy had gonorrhea, instead of calling our office to clarify why Darcy's test results would be left on *Marcy's* cellphone, she TEXTED her sister the following message: "You have gonorrhea. You and Ryan need to get to Dr. Burbank's office for treatment right away."

Needless to say, Darcy was understandably upset to receive the news in such a tacky, unprofessional manner. Instead of calling us to clarify things, however, Darcy texted her boyfriend, Ryan, and raked him over the coals for cheating on her and inflicting her with gonorrhea. Ryan insisted he'd never cheated and she was the only partner he'd ever had. Darcy didn't believe him and broke off their relationship.

Upon further reflection, though, Darcy called our office and was curious how we'd made the diagnosis of gonorrhea on her since she'd only come in for her Gardasil vaccine. "Can you get gonorrhea from a vaccine?" she inquired. Okay, let's be frank— neither of these girls ranked as class valedictorian.

My medical assistant scratched her head. Why did Darcy think she had gonorrhea when *her sister* was the one who had the infection? And no, Darcy, you cannot get gonorrhea from a vaccine!

Once my medical assistant figured out what happened, we called Marcy and told her she and her boyfriend were the ones who needed treatment, *not* Darcy and Ryan!

Here's where things got dicey. Marcy wanted to delay coming in for treatment until she could sleep with her boyfriend and transmit the disease to him!

Why? Turns out, she did not show symptoms of gonorrhea until she'd had too much to drink and impulsively participated in a one-night stand with a guy she barely knew. The boyfriend didn't know, and she hadn't had sex with him since cheating on him. Thus, if the Health Department tested him right now, he would test negative for the infection, and then he'd find out she'd cheated on him and obtained her STD from some other guy.

In short, Marcy wanted him to test positive so she could blame her infection on his *ex-girlfriend*! She'd claim his ex infected him, and then he'd infected her.

Had someone transported me to Peyton Place?

I told her to get her gonorrhea-infected self into my office *now* and not after she'd slept with her boyfriend! The whole mess reminded me of a favorite quote:

> *"Oh, what a tangled web we weave,*
> *when first we practice to deceive."*
>
> ~SIR WALTER SCOTT

Bizarre

Munchausen's Syndrome

Some of the most challenging patients to diagnose and treat are those who self-inflict injuries to gain attention and sympathy.

Sharon Mason was such a patient. She came in to see me with an infected, dime-sized ulcer on the side of her tongue. I assumed she had bitten it, and the site had become infected. I instructed her to gargle with Listerine three times a day, and I prescribed an antibiotic.

The ulcer almost completely healed over the next several weeks but then came back with a vengeance. I screened for lupus and Behçet's syndrome and cultured for herpes simplex virus, but results were negative. When the ulcer grew even larger two months later, I shook my head, stumped. I'd never seen anything like it, and since it was a non-healing sore, I worried she might have cancer of the tongue. I referred her to an oral surgeon to biopsy the lesion.

YOU'LL NEED THAT PATCH FROM NOW ON. NEXT TIME, REMEMBER TO SNEEZE INTO YOUR **ARM** ...

offthemark.com

Imagine my shock when the surgeon called me after the office visit and said the ulcer margins were too crisp for cancer. He suspected it was self-inflicted!

What?

Yup! He confronted her and unbelievably, Sharon had *intentionally* hacked off chunks of her tongue with dirty kitchen scissors to gain medical attention—a condition known as Munchausen's syndrome. Even more amazing? This older oral surgeon had seen one other case of intentional tongue hacking in his thirty-year career!

In a more serious case of Munchausen, a local nurse repeatedly showed up in the emergency room with plummeting blood pressures and temperatures over 103 degrees—a condition known as septic shock. At every hospitalization, her blood cultures grew out *E. coli* bacteria.

Normally, *E. coli* sepsis is caused by a kidney infection that seeds bacteria into the bloodstream, but this woman's urine never cultured positive for *E. coli*. So how was it getting into her blood? We performed a colonoscopy to see if she had colon lesions that seeded bacteria into her blood stream. No. Her colon was healthy. What was going on?

The case was clenched when her coworkers rushed her to my office one Friday after she'd been healthy for over three months. While performing her physical exam, I happened to notice a fresh puncture wound on her left inner-elbow crease. Surrounding the puncture was a large hematoma, like she had started an IV but then collapsed it. Since she had not had blood drawn or an IV started in over three months, no reasonable explanation existed for the new puncture wound—*unless she herself had poked in the needle to infuse something.*

When I questioned her about the puncture wound, she because defensive and offered a lame excuse: a mosquito bit her.

In January? Do I look like I fell off a turnip truck? Her defensiveness and lack of eye contact only raised my suspicion.

After consulting with an infectious disease specialist, we ordered a subtype culture analysis that confirmed the *E. coli* in her blood matched that of her own feces. Thus, we proved the *E. coli* was *not* caused by an outside source such as a food poisoning, and with her punctured arm, we clinched the case.

When confronted about her self-inflicted illness, she initially denied it and flew into a rage. Eventually, however, a psychiatrist dragged out of her exactly what she'd done. Turns out, she contaminated bags of intravenous fluid *with a liquefied form of her own feces,* and then infused the murky, *E. coli*-laden fluid into her veins, thereby inducing septic shock.

Like most Munchausen patients, Sharon didn't *want* to get better. She craved the pity and attention and flowers she received from friends and co-workers whenever she went into the hospital. Thus, once we were on to her schemes, she switched doctors and hospitals.

Munchausen patients are challenging to diagnose, as most of us can't imagine willfully cutting off chunks of our own tongues or injecting feces into our veins. Most Munchausen patients were neglected as children and often *only* received attention when they were sick. This can trigger certain patients to self-induce illness to glean attention or pity. Most will adamantly deny self-inflicting their injury, and when confronted, become hostile and defensive. Like Sharon, they'll then switch doctors and repeat the cycle again.

The saddest cases are Munchausen-by-proxy, where a parent inflicts injury on her child or baby, but then dashes the child to the health care provider and plays the role of the caring, worried, long-suffering mother. She gains attention through her sick child. The things some people do to get attention!

"Work hard for a cause, not for applause. Live life to express, not to impress. Don't strive to make your presence noticed, just make your absence felt."

~ AUTHOR UNKNOWN

Please, *Not* in the Waiting Room!

At times, Billie Yardley exemplified odd behavior, very odd behavior. Case in point: One day, he sauntered up to my receptionist stating he needed to be examined right away for a diabetic leg ulcer. Since Billie arrived for his appointment thirty minutes early, and two other patients preceded him on the schedule, the receptionist asked him to take a seat.

Instead of sitting down, however, Billie wandered around the waiting room, at times staring into space, and at other times, smacking and licking his lips in a noisy, peculiar fashion. He then insisted he could smell burning rubber and asked the other patients in the waiting room if they could, too.

"I don't smell anything," the woman nearest him said, no doubt thinking, *What a weird duck!*

Suddenly, Billie yanked off his polo shirt, unhitched his belt, and tugged his pants clear down to his feet. There he stood, clad only in his Fruit of the Loom undies, as though this was the most natural thing in the world. Perhaps if he'd had the physique of Tom Cruise instead of Santa Claus, the other patients in the waiting room might have protested less—but I doubt it.

Someone came up to the front desk and notified my receptionist of Billie's unsettling behavior. She pointed at our new underwear model and whispered, "I just thought you ought to know."

One glance at Billie standing in the middle of a packed waiting room dressed only in his underwear, and my receptionist's eyes bulged in horror. She dashed to his side. "Mr. Yardley! What are you doing? You can't undress out here!"

As though in a trance, he said, "Dr. Burbank needs to see this sore on my leg." He pointed at a small, denuded ulcer on his shin.

"But we can't have patients out here in their underwear."

He shrugged. "Why not? She usually runs behind, so I figured I'd save her some time by having my clothes off already." He glanced around the waiting room at the other patients and suggested, "You know, if you other patients did the same thing, she'd get through a lot quicker."

The patients all stared at him scandalized, and then turned toward my brand new receptionist to see how she would handle the waiting-room exhibitionist.

Sweat poured from her brow as she tried not to panic. Something was terribly "off" with Mr. Yardley (and she didn't mean just his trousers), so no point trying to reason with him. She pulled up his trousers, curled her arm through his, and attempted to escort him back to an exam room. "Let's get you into an exam room so Dr. Burbank can take a look at the sore, shall we?"

Billie would have none of it. "Naw, I'd rather see Dr. Burbank here. It's less cramped here in the waiting room than in those dinky exam rooms of hers."

Now desperate, my receptionist said, "HIPAA law forbids doctors from examining patients in their underwear in the waiting room. You wouldn't want Dr. Burbank to do something illegal and get into trouble, would you?"

Technically, nowhere in the HIPAA privacy law did it specifically ban me from examining a patient in his underwear in the waiting room—I just can't say the patient's *name* or give *medical advice* while I do it! Since no other patient had ever requested an undressed waiting room examination before, her statement sounded legit.

Tired of fooling around with his shenanigans, she grabbed his arm and bodily dragged him back to an examination room as the other patients in the waiting room snickered, elbowed one another, and whispered, "He must have a screw loose."

No, Billie does not have a screw loose, nor is he an exhibitionist or pervert. Billie displayed the classic signs and symptoms of complex partial seizures, or temporal lobe epilepsy, a condition that makes patients do bizarre behaviors, such as lip smacking, staring, and wandering around as though sleepwalking. Déjà vu and visual and smell hallucinations are common. Patients often become argumentative and combative. After the seizure is over, they have no memory of what they said or did.

Poor Billie has engaged in other strange behaviors over the years. One time, he wandered around a restaurant stabbing his fork into the meatballs and ravioli of complete strangers. He meandered from table to table, sampling the entrees and declaring the food delicious.

Needless to say, the other patrons were aghast and complained to the waitress who then notified the manager. In the middle of his seizure, of course, Billie saw nothing wrong with nibbling from the plates of complete strangers. He argued with the waitress and manager. "I just wanted a teeny, tiny taste to see if I'd want to order the meatballs or ravioli myself next time," he explained. "I don't see why the woman made such a fuss—I left her five meatballs."

Since Billie retains no recollection of his dreadful behavior once the seizure is over, he only learned about his offensive manners when the police showed up to escort him out of the restaurant. Thankfully, by then he'd come out of his seizure and didn't argue with the cop!

Billie works as a cashier in a Mom and Pop hardware store. During one seizure, while trying to make change for a twenty-dollar bill, he stuffed the money into his own pants pocket and told the customer *he* needed the money more than the customer! When the customer complained to the manager, the manager thankfully recognized Billie's telltale lip smacking and bizarre behavior and knew his long-term employee was having a seizure and wasn't a thief. He quickly gave the customer his change and smoothed things over by explaining Billie's condition to the customer. Since Billie's seizures were rare, and Billie was otherwise a top-notch employee, his boss tolerated his occasional epileptic fits.

To his credit, Billie has not allowed epilepsy to ruin his life. While I would be mortified to find out I'd wandered around a doctor's waiting room in my underwear or stabbed meatballs right off the plates of other diners, Billie has a wonderful attitude. After we informed him he'd wandered around our office in his whitey-tighties, he shook his head and roared with laughter. "Wait 'til Annie (his wife) hears about this."

In fact, Billie's attitude was so good, he told me seizure jokes at every visit. This one was my favorite:

Q. *What do you call an epileptic in the garden?*
A. *A Seizure Salad*

Billie exemplifies my all-time favorite saying:

> *"If you don't like something, change it. If you can't change it, change your attitude."*
>
> ~ MAYA ANGELOU

One Way to Induce Seizures

In twenty-five years of practicing medicine, I have found manic patients who refuse to take their medications my most challenging patients. Take, for example, seventy-year-old Elijah Crane. He started off his new patient appointment by informing me he had fired his last five doctors because *they* were all crazy. Swell! No doubt, I'd soon rank as his sixth crazy doctor.

"Ain't nothing wrong with me," he insisted, arms crossed defiantly. "*They're* the ones with the problem."

I inquired what specific behaviors had worried the previous doctors. He mentioned motorcycle racing in an ice storm, his request for Viagra when his wife was still recovering from hip surgery, and his compulsive yard sale buying. In fact, he'd purchased so much junk at his most recent garage sale it wouldn't fit into his garage. Furthermore, his spending sprees left no money for food or electricity.

LET ME GET THIS STRAIGHT, IT'S BEEN TWO CONSECUTIVE HOURS SINCE YOU'VE SLEPT?

offthemark.com

ATLANTIC FEATURE © 1993 MARK PARISI

MARK PARISI

WHEN CATS EXPERIENCE INSOMNIA

When he mentioned he hadn't slept in three nights straight and that he planned a trip to Washington, DC, (on his motorcycle in the middle of the winter) to personally meet with President Obama and tell him how to run the country, his last doctor tried to talk him into a voluntary admission to the psych ward. Elijah would have none of it and charged out of the office after cussing out the doctor.

Yup! This guy was manic, all right!

After listening to his non-stop rant for over an hour without getting a word in edgewise, I knew enough not to use the words bi-polar or manic, or he'd just get mad and storm out. Thus, I told him he had a chemical imbalance that needed immediate care. I secretly hoped he'd steamroll out of my office because I could tell already he would be a high-maintenance patient.

No such luck.

Instead, he developed a huge crush on me and started bringing me gifts. Weird gifts: dirty canning jars; a rusty, broken alarm clock; a 1987 wall calendar; and a book about motorcycles. Was he just unloading the junk that would no longer fit in his garage, or was this his idea of a gift?

The insanity reached a climax the day he marched into my office with what looked like an eight-foot-long log he'd cut in half lengthwise and sanded into a massive wall hanging. On it, he had installed a broken clock, a blown-up photo of his two granddaughters in their pink tutus, and a hand-painted pine tree drawn with the skill of a toddler. In the tree, he had decoupaged pictures of birds cut out of magazines. Some of the birds were half the size of the tree, and others were tiny. The overall effect? Dreadful. Laughable. Crazier than Squeaky Fromme and Charles Manson combined.

He yanked down the framed and matted prints of Monet and Cezanne that graced my waiting room walls and began pounding in nails and brackets, fully intending to mount his monstrosity in their place. When my receptionist protested, he argued with her. "Dr. Burbank has had those same two pictures on her walls since the first day I came here. Time she got something new, so I'm giving her this." He gestured toward his wooden eyesore and looked as proud as a preschooler with a fistful of dandelions. My receptionist dashed back to my office and shoved me into the waiting room.

I could feel my eyes bulging out of my head as I stared at his horrendous wall hanging, now fully mounted onto the wall. *Was I on* Candid Camera? I glanced around the room hoping for a hidden camera, but instead, I only saw patients snickering and whispering to each other. Others stared at me, no doubt watching to see how I'd handle the situation.

With as much enthusiasm as I could muster I said, "Wow! What a unique wall hanging. I've never seen anything quite like it."

"That's 'cause I made it myself," he said, grinning like he'd painted the Mona Lisa.

I then told him the pink of his granddaughters' tutus clashed with the dusty rose paint on my walls, so I'd have to hang it somewhere else. I assured him I'd find a special place for it . . . the local dump came to mind!

After work that night, I hung the monstrosity in the lobby outside my office and contemplated how to get rid of it without hurting his feelings. As the staff and I stared at the garish thing, we joked that perhaps we could say since it was made of wood, it posed a fire hazard, or it was so heavy it might conk a patient on the head and cause a concussion. Could we bribe the cleaning crew to "steal" it?

Suddenly, my receptionist slunk to the floor and shook like she was having a grand mal seizure. Taking the cue I laughed and commented, "I get it, we'll tell him it's so hideous it triggers seizures."

When my receptionist started turning blue, grinding her teeth, and shaking so hard I couldn't arouse her, I realized she wasn't acting!

She was actually having a grand mal seizure!

We rolled her onto her side, protected her tongue and airway, and when her seizure was over, we wheeled her straight to the ER for evaluation. She had never had a seizure before, nor has she had one since. Clearly, the wall hanging posed a serious health hazard: grand mal seizures! What a pity it had to go!

"A question that sometimes drives me hazy: am I or are the others crazy?"

~ ALBERT EINSTEIN

R2-D2 is a Doctor?

While visiting her parents in rural Kentucky, Stephanie developed a nasty stomach virus which caused non-stop diarrhea and vomiting. After nearly passing out on her way to the bathroom, she knew she'd become severely dehydrated and needed IV fluids.

Her husband drove her to the tiny twenty-bed hospital near her mother's home, but instead of being examined by a bona-fide emergency room doctor, this hospital only employed a RO-BOT in the middle of the night.

A technician linked Stephanie via Skype to a doctor in England (where it was daytime) who obtained the details of her illness. Next, a robot obtained her vital signs and "examined" her heart, lungs, and abdomen using the metal sensor on its "hand." This information was transmitted to the doctor in England who provided a diagnosis and treatment plan. After she'd received IV fluids and nausea medication, Stephanie was discharged.

offthemark.com   ATLANTIC FEATURE © 2000 MARK PARISI

TURN YOUR HEAD AND COUGH

MARK PARISI

WHY "VIRTUAL DOCTOR" NEVER CAUGHT ON

She shook her head, still in shock about her unusual ER visit. "I thought I must be delirious when this huge robot thing with blinking eyes and mechanical arms started examining me. The technician called him 'Dr. Robbie.' I asked when a real doctor would be in to examine me, but he informed me Dr. Robbie was the only "doctor" available until six in the morning. I couldn't believe my ears! A robot performing my abdominal exam? Would a robot be able to distinguish a stomach bug from appendicitis? It freaked me out, but what else could I do in the middle of the night, in the middle of nowhere?"

Amazingly, the patient received the same treatment from "Dr. Robbie" that she would have received from me.

I'm not too worried robots will replace me completely, however. Can you imagine enduring a rectal or pelvic exam performed by a robot with eight-inch long metal fingers? Since robots lack emotion, they wouldn't flinch (or stop) when you howled in pain!

"My computer beat me at checkers,
but I sure beat it at kickboxing."

~ AUTHOR UNKNOWN

Pregnancy and
the Lack
Thereof

An *Expensive* Way to Diagnose Pregnancy

In my first year of practice, a college student came in because she hadn't had her menstrual cycle in two months, and this was very unusual for her. "Normally, it comes on like clockwork every month," she insisted.

Of course, my first question? "Could you possibly be pregnant?"

"Absolutely not," she said, shaking her head emphatically. "I broke up with my boyfriend a long, long time ago. I haven't had sex in like, forever."

Hmmm. My brain rattled off the differential: stress, polycystic ovary disease, hormone imbalance, thyroid disease, ovarian cyst or mass, and endometriosis. I ordered a pelvic ultrasound and some blood tests.

Imagine my embarrassment when two days later, the radiolo-

"Well... I think we should run a pregnancy test. Just to make sure!"

gist called to inform me the patient had an eight-week-old fetus with a viable heartbeat growing inside her!

I felt like a fool. I'd ordered an expensive pelvic ultrasound when a four-dollar pregnancy test would have sufficed!

I clenched my teeth and fumed. She had insisted she couldn't possibly be pregnant since she hadn't had sex in "forever." When I called to inform her she was pregnant, she confirmed that yes, she and her ex-boyfriend had indeed had unprotected sex about eight weeks earlier, shortly before they'd broken up.

Apparently, her definition of a long, long time and forever were decidedly different from mine!

I learned my lesson. Now when a high school or college girl claims she can't possibly be pregnant, I still run a pregnancy test to be sure. I have picked up at least a dozen pregnancies over the years in girls who claimed they were virgins or used condoms every time. Only after informing them of the positive pregnancy results did they confess, "Well, there was that one time . . . "

"Pickles and ice cream? No! The most common craving of pregnant women is not to be pregnant."

~ PHYLLIS DILLER

A Cure for Teen Pregnancy?

Nothing triggers more angst in a mother than the thought of her teenaged daughter becoming pregnant. This was especially true for Tamela, a patient with a checkered past.

By age sixteen, Tamela had been with more sexual partners than she could count. She didn't even know the names of some of the guys she'd slept with. "I was drunk or stoned all the time, so those years were a blur." Her alcoholic parents provided no boundaries or supervision, so she was a classic case of "looking for love in all the wrong places." Too immature to take birth control pills responsibly, she aborted three babies before the age of twenty.

In her mid-twenties she met a great guy who loved her and treated her with respect. She gladly abandoned her promiscuous ways, and soon, they were married. The couple joined a church and found friends in a young married couples class.

All was well until Tamela became a mother, and her daughter started her first menstrual cycle at age ten. Petrified that her daughter would repeat her wanton ways and end up pregnant, Tamela scheduled an appointment for her

MOM! DAD! I JUST FOUND OUT I'M GOING TO BE A MOTHER!

KATE REALLY SHOULD HAVE TOLD HER PARENTS ABOUT TRYING OUT FOR THE SCHOOL PLAY

offthemark.com

©2010 MARK PARISI DIST. BY UFS INC.

daughter to come discuss birth control with me.

I walked into the exam room and faced Chavel, a young girl with huge, terrified eyes. She was gripping the arms of her chair and visibly shaking. Turns out, the mother wanted me to inject a Provera shot into her daughter today—and every three months—to keep her from getting pregnant. The poor girl grabbed my arm and begged, "Please don't give me a shot. I don't need it. I don't do that nasty stuff."

Not only was Chavel not sexually active, she didn't even *like* boys yet. Instead, she preferred to hang out with her girl friends. "Don't you have to sleep with a boy to get pregnant?" she whimpered. "It doesn't make sense to give me a shot if I'm not doing the nasty."

Her mother was adamant, however. She wanted no chance of her daughter getting pregnant.

Eyes pooling with tears, Chavel hurled at her mother, "Just cause you were a slut doesn't mean I'll be one."

At an impasse, the two glared at one another then turned to face me, arms crossed. Swell!

I decided, right or wrong, that the mother was projecting onto her daughter her own neglected and unsupervised childhood. Just because she'd chosen promiscuity at a young age didn't mean her daughter was predestined to follow in her footsteps; Chavel was growing up in an entirely different home environment, with two involved parents who loved her, and obviously weren't afraid to have "the talk." Plus, Chavel attended a Christian school where the norm was definitely not sexual activity at age ten! Chavel, with the candor of youth, insisted, "I ain't letting no boy stick his 'thingy' in me when he might have just peed out of it. Eeww!"

I had a frank discussion with Chavel about Tamela's childhood and how much she regretted the poor choices she'd made.

She didn't want her daughter to follow in her painful path. We talked about taking responsibility for your choices.

In the end, we all reached an agreement that Chavel wouldn't have to endure the injections as long as she was a virgin and not even dating. I expressed my personal opinion that her best choice would be to remain a virgin until marriage, but if she chose to become sexually active, she needed to take responsibility for her choice and to use birth control and condoms to prevent STDs.

Chavel promised she would notify us if she were even close to sexual activity. She knew her mom and I thought remaining a virgin was her best choice, but she didn't have to "sneak around" if she chose otherwise. She promised she'd be responsible.

As they exited the exam room, I prayed Chavel wasn't lying and that her mother wouldn't sue me if Chavel ended up pregnant at twelve!

I'm happy to report Chavel graduated from high school and college still a virgin (or so she claimed); she later married a wonderful guy from church.

Perhaps her mother's "scare tactics" had worked after all! Wave a huge needle and syringe in a young girl's face with the threat that if she even thinks about having sex, mom will demand she get a shot in the butt every three months. It worked like a charm, though who knows if Chavel will end up in therapy someday from the emotional trauma she endured at age ten.

"If you have never been hated by your child, you have never been a parent."

~ BETTE DAVIS

A Lousy Aphrodisiac

WARNING: This story contains graphic medical descriptions
guaranteed to gross out all male readers!

Unlike Tamela, who was terrified her daughter might become pregnant, Maggie, a married housewife, was desperate to become a mother, but so far she'd had no success in getting pregnant. (Maybe she should schedule an appointment with Chavel's mother instead of her gynecologist, as she sure had no trouble conceiving!)

Maggie had gone off birth control more than a year ago, and at age thirty-eight, she feared her internal clock would soon "tick out." Her monthly cycles were somewhat erratic, so she wondered if she was even ovulating. Thus, I taught her how to tell when she was ovulating based on what her cervical mucus looked like at each stage of the cycle. "Right at ovulation, the mucus thins out into a clear, egg-whitish consistency that will maintain a two-inch string when you pull your fingers apart," I explained. "When you see that thin, clear discharge, *that* is your most fertile time. That is when you should have relations with your husband."

Armed with her new secret, Maggie became an expert at deciphering when she was about to ovulate. Unfortunately, her skills at seducing her husband left a lot to be desired.

One Saturday, when her husband was glued to ESPN cheering for his alma mater in a pivotal football game against an archrival, Maggie noticed while in the bathroom her cervical mucus confirmed she was about to ovulate. So excited the magic moment had arrived, she barged into the living room and announced to her husband, in the middle of the third quar-

FERTILITY TREATMENT FOR
SEEDLESS WATERMELONS

ter of his game, "Look! My cervical mucus shows I'm ovulating!" She marched up to his La-Z-Boy and demonstrated—just inches from his face—how the clear goo would string out several inches.

She apparently expected him to flip cartwheels of excitement over her recent discovery, preferably in the direction of their bedroom. Instead, he stared at the sickening slime, turned pale, and yanked his head back as though she'd swung a dead mouse in his face. *Yuk! Why did she think he wanted an up-close visual of her bodily secretions?*

"I'm ovulating," she announced proudly, a grin plastered on her face. "See? It strings out a full two inches," she said, demonstrating her magic trick again. "We've got to go do it right now!" She yanked on his arm and demanded he fulfill his marital duties before it was too late.

He eyed the television wistfully and her nasty mucus in disgust. Did she seriously think he'd be in the mood in the middle of the most exciting game of the season? The score was tied!

Not taking the hint, she upped the ante with a guilt-trip: "What's more important, our baby or some dumb football game?"

He relented, if only to appease her and get back to his game as quickly as possible. Unfortunately, his anger at her for interrupting his game, coupled with his queasy stomach from her sickening mucus display, rendered him impotent for the first time in their marriage. She huffed out of the bedroom, frustrated he had ruined a prime opportunity to conceive. He huffed out sputtering she had spoiled his game and treated him like nothing more than a sperm donor.

Maggie told me about their disastrous encounter at her next appointment. I reminded her she had *twelve hours* after seeing the first signs of ovulation to maintain top fertility. I suggested that in the future, she let him finish his game, *then* slip on a sexy negligee—and come up with a better aphrodisiac than cervical mucus! Soft music and candles, perhaps? "Let the status of your secretions remain *our* little secret."

She laughed and agreed her seduction techniques could stand a little finesse. The advice must have worked, because within a year she had conceived a beautiful baby boy.

"How delightful is your love, my bride! How much more pleasing is your love than wine, and the fragrance of your perfume than any spice!"

~ SONG OF SOLOMON 4:10 (NIV)

Outrageous
and More
Outrageous!

Codes, Codes, and *More* Codes!

Thumbing through the ICD-9 book of diagnostic codes is an eye-opening experience. For starters, who needs a code for "hit by a nuclear bomb?" Will the patient or doctor need to worry about a proper Medicare ICD-9 code if a nuclear holocaust occurs? And how often does a patient survive a head-on collision with an oncoming train? Come to think of it, I haven't used code E832—patient forced off a gangplank—in the last few centuries either.

Then there are the diseases I've never heard of: Dumdum fever (085.0) and Twiddler's syndrome (996.04).

Some codes are vague. For example, when my husband forgets the milk I reminded him to pick up on his way home from work, does code 317 for "feeble-minded" apply? When my sister loses ten pounds but I gain ten, does that constitute code 313.3—sibling jealousy disorder?

Some codes we pray we'll never need, such as code E876.6—procedure performed on *wrong patient* or code V15.80—*failed anesthesia*. Yikes! Apparently, patients *do* wake up in the middle of their bypass surgeries!

How about code E876.7? *Wrong body part removed.* You go in for a new knee and come out with a new hip! Or the *wrong side* code. You go in for a RIGHT mastectomy and wake up with your LEFT breast cut off. Can you spell L-A-W-S-U-I-T?

Some codes are politically incorrect. We all know never to call a mentally-challenged person a "retard," but the ICD-9 coding book still uses the old, insulting codes for low-IQ patients: moron, imbecile, and idiot. (In case you're wondering, it's better to be a moron than an idiot.) Even if you're an intellectual giant, the coding book may still label you with code 301.7, *moral imbecile.*

Now that we are converting to electronic medical records, do you want code 784.99 for fetid breath or code 787.3 for flatulence to be prominently displayed on your problem list for the doctors and nurses of every specialty to see? Or what if a harried doctor hits an errant number key, and your medical record now labels you as a necrophiliac (someone who likes sex with dead people), or worse yet, a coprophiliac (code 302.89). Don't know what that means? Trust me, you don't want to know!

Most of the codes seem bureaucratic. Does *how* you sprain your ankle (playing rugby, soccer, football, dodgeball, water polo, cricket, ultimate Frisbee, bungee jumping, dancing, or cheerleading) really matter? No, but the codebook has a separate code for EACH of these sports, even though I'll use rest, ice, ACE wraps, and elevation on your swollen ankle regardless of how you sprained it.

Likewise, who cares if I get kicked in the head while *milking* a goat (E019.0) versus *shearing* a goat (E019.2)? Isn't the important thing how much damage the goat's hoof does to my brain? Who cares if it's a moose, horse and buggy, or telephone pole my bicycle crashes into? (Well, the moose might care!) But you guessed it; ICD-9 provides a separate code for each, based on *what* I crash into!

What about that code for fertile eunuch syndrome (257.2)?

Isn't a *fertile eunuch*, by definition, an oxymoron?

Now that Medicare is cracking down on fraud, will I be sent to jail if I code a patient with a tapeworm as having a hookworm, roundworm, or pinworm? Will I be slapped with a hefty fine if I accidentally code a patient with Rocky Mountain spotted fever using the Colorado tick code instead of the Rocky Mountain tick code? If so, do all Colorado ticks know the state boundary lines?

Things are soon to get worse. In October of 2015, Medicare is mandating we use its new ICD-10 coding book, adding **55,000** *additional* codes. Thanks to ICD-10, I'll have to decipher between 750 different codes just to code for a fractured hip!

I can see it now: I'll have to document the number of horns on Bullwinkle's antlers when I crash into him on my bicycle. When I fracture my ankle falling off a flagpole (yes, there is a code for that—E882), they'll want to know *which state's flag* was flying from said flagpole and if the flag was at full or half-mast!

A new code should be implemented for the frustration I feel: Physician Coding Anxiety disorder. I propose this code be SOS.

"*Every revolution evaporates and leaves behind only the slime of a new bureaucracy.*"

~FRANZ KAFKA

Grandma Got Run
Over by a *Reindeer*

Since implementing a plan to reduce our country's seventeen trillion dollar national debt has proven too politically taxing for our current Congress, they have instead mandated the use of 55,000 new medical diagnostic codes called ICD-10. After all, what's more important: preventing our nation from financial collapse or having the proper diagnostic code for "Crushed by a falling alligator (Code W58.03A)?

How did I practice medicine all these years without code W56.11A (bit by a sea lion)? Next time a patient stabs herself with a crochet needle, I'll be ready (code Y93D1).

But I ask you: if an unfortunate patient gets *"sucked into a jet engine,"* will he live to *care* if I've picked code V97.33A?

I *will* hand it to Congress on one thing—while they don't have the resolve to prevent Social Security and Medicare insolvency, they *did* plan ahead for the eventual soul who "collides with a spaceship" (code V95.43).

Remember the silly Christmas song, "Grandma Got Run Over by a Reindeer?" Thanks to ICD-10, a proper code now exists for this unfortunate calamity: W55.32A.

Here are some of the other codes I am expected to use come

October 2015:

> Struck by a falling turkey: W61.42A
> Bit by an Orca whale: W56.21A
> Burn due to water skis on fire: V91.07A (How is this possible?)
> Walked into a lamppost: W22.02A
> Walked into a lamppost, *second time*: W22.02D
> Walked into a lamppost, *subsequent times:* W22.02S (For the truly clueless and clumsy!)
> Asphyxiated in a discarded refrigerator at the dump: T71.231A
> Lips stuck to a tuba: Y93.J4
> Drowned in a bucket of water: W16.221A
> Horseback rider collides with trolley: V80.730A

Luckily, for those hectic days when I can't be bothered to take a decent medical history (because I'm too busy looking up diagnostic codes!), here is the best code of all:

Y34 (*Un*specified event, *un*specified place, *un*specified time, and *un*determined intention).

Here's the irony of that code—the whole *reason* they came up with all the new ICD-10 codes is to force us doctors to become MORE specific with our coding! Go figure!

"Paperwork is the embalming fluid of bureaucracy, maintaining an appearance of life where none exists."

~ ROBERT MELTZER

The Downside of Electronic Medical Records

The federal government is pushing doctors to convert from paper charts to electronic medical records. I recently tried out a program that would allow me to dictate my notes verbally, and a computer would automatically type my dictation into a printed office note. It sounded like something even a techno-challenged individual like me could handle! I was gung ho and ready to sign on the dotted line until I attended a yearly malpractice prevention conference on the legal dangers now showing up because of electronic medical records. Voice recognition software, it seems, carries legal risks. Take, for example, the following doctor dictations erroneously transcribed by the computer:

Patient was *prepped and raped* in the usual fashion. (Should have read "prepped and draped.")

Exam of the toddler's genitals revealed they were *circus-sized.* ("circumcised")

Laboratory tests revealed abnormal *lover* function. ("liver")

Patient was *fouled up* by the neurologist. ("followed up")

Patient died because of *sixty-eight chefs.* ("CHF = congestive heart failure")

His headaches began *when you're a goat.* ("one year ago")

Patient is still under the *car* of the physical therapist. ("care")—No wonder the patient needs PT!

The patient was *X-rated* after a thorough exam by the doctor. ("X-rayed")

The pharmacist made an error in *copulation*. ("calculation")

Patient agreed to try *home anal replacement* therapy. ("hormonal")

An echocardiogram will be performed to rule out a *paint and frame valley*. ("patent foramen ovale")

The patient was discharged with *homo two*. ("home O2 = home oxygen)

Suspect *purple muscular* disease. ("peripheral vascular disease")

Will carefully monitor *eyes and nose*. ("I's and O's," which means input and output of fluid and urine)

The patient needed several rounds of *Kaye Ciel*. ("KCl = potassium chloride")

The patient endured a protracted hospital stay from a *staff* infection in his *baloney amputation*. ("Staph" and "below-knee amputation")

Patient's foot was cold and pulseless, with a *purple shoe*. ("purplish hue")

Patient was admitted to the Psychiatric ward after exhibiting *bazaar* behavior. ("bizarre"—Too much shopping, perhaps?)

The orthopedic said surgery would not help the patient's degenerative *dick* disease. ("disc")

When asked why he insisted on going home from the hospital against his doctor's advice, the patient replied, *"I just want to live."* ("leave"— In some hospitals, the patients may have to leave to live!)

The *SOB* has improved. ("shortness of breath")

Hmm. Maybe I'll stick with my paper patient charts after all!

Outrageous Insurance Company Decisions

The CEOs of most medical insurance companies rake in huge salaries, so nothing infuriates me more than when a patient is denied a medically necessary procedure because "Big Brother" deems it unnecessary. Big Brother, I might add, is often just some twerp in Bangalore, India, who knows as much about the medical field as I do about aerospace engineering. Despite his thick, nearly unintelligible accent, he informs me his name is "Bruce" or "George." Right, and I am Mahatma Gandhi!

Sometimes their responses are so absurd I have to threaten them with a complaint to the Department of Insurance. Requesting the *exact spelling* of the employee's name so I can include him in my lawsuit works the best at persuading "Bruce" to see things my way.

Case in point: A patient of mine had such baggy upper eye lids the droopy skin fell over her eyes and interfered with her vision. She also complained her eyes felt heavy and tired all the time. After consulting with a plastic surgeon, we called to obtain an insurance authorization for surgery to remove the

THE HMO REVIEW BOARD

12795 DAYS WITHOUT ACCIDENTALLY APPROVING A CLAIM

sagging upper eyelid skin. Imagine our disgust when her insurance company responded that they would only pay for *one eye* to be done. Thus, one eye would look perky, youthful, and wrinkle-free, while the other would look even more droopy and saggy in comparison. The end result? She'd look like a freak—a Cyclops.

Another patient developed an aggressive form of breast cancer necessitating a bilateral mastectomy. Just thirty-four years of age and single, she obtained breast implants. Unfortunately, after several years, one of the implants ruptured, and she was left with a lemon-sized blob of implant capsule unnaturally heaped on the side of her chest. She couldn't wear any snug-fitting tops or swim suits without feeling self-conscious.

I applied to have her ruptured implant removed and a new one inserted to match the size of her other implant. Her insurance company, however, refused to pay for a surgeon to remove the blob of silicon "unless the pain is so unbearable she requires narcotic pain medications to control it."

Fuming, I called the medical director to appeal the decision. My patient shouldn't have to take pain pills for the rest of her life when the ruptured implant could easily be removed and replaced. His response? "Fine, we'll pay to remove the ruptured implant *but not to replace it.*"

What? I argued with him: "She's only thirty-four years old. She can't walk around the beach with one breast a size 38D and the other as flat as the Kansas prairie. She's already had to face breast cancer, chemotherapy, baldness, and bilateral mastectomies . . . isn't that enough? How can you leave her emotionally traumatized and feeling like a circus freak?"

He blew me off. "Bust size is not my concern," he said smugly. "I run an insurance company, not a Miss America pageant, and replacing that implant would be purely cosmetic; I won't approve it."

What a jerk! My patient couldn't afford to replace the implant herself. What galled me most was just hours later, this same medical director approved a male patient's prescription for Viagra with no hassle whatsoever! Grrr!

"When all is said and done, more is said than done."

~ AESOP

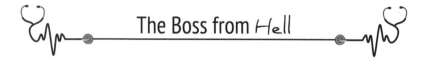

The Boss from Hell

Rita Lawson had managed the medical office of Dr. Frankel for twenty-eight years. Twenty-eight *long* years.

Dr. Frankel's idea of a generous Christmas bonus was a dinky box with four bath oil beads from Walmart. She hadn't received a raise since Bush was in office. Bush Senior, that is. Even then, he'd only dished out a paltry twenty-five cents an hour. Despite coming in early and leaving late with no paid overtime because she was a salaried position, never once had he said, "Thank you." Why had she put up with the ungrateful Scrooge for so long? Undeserved loyalty? Habit? Masochism? Sheer stupidity?

In twenty-eight years, she had only missed two days of work—for a severe vomiting bug. Even then, her boss said, "If I'd known you just had a little stomach virus, I could have injected you with a shot of Phenergan and hooked you up to a bag of IV fluids right here in the office. Then you wouldn't

"If you work 24 hours a day, you won't need your apartment and that will save you a lot of money and that's the same as getting a raise!"

have gotten two days behind with your work." He patted her shoulder. "Don't worry, I'm sure you'll catch up on your work this weekend." He then scrubbed his hands with Germ-X while sputtering how he hoped he didn't catch her infection.

When Dr. Frankel added a new medical partner, did he add another receptionist to help her with the increased workload? Of course not! Instead, he heaped the added piles of work on her desk and made a half-baked stab at humor: "You should thank me for this. Now you won't have time to get into trouble."

Ha, ha, ha, she sputtered under her breath, waiting until he left the room to pound her desk.

Things reached a climax when Rita's gallbladder misbehaved, and she needed an urgent cholecystectomy. Not surprisingly, the first words out of Dr. Frankel's mouth when she called to inform him why she hadn't made it into work? "What a lousy time to get sick. You have to get the office Christmas cards out by Friday so they don't arrive late."

She felt like slamming down the phone on the uncaring old codger! Here she lay in the hospital, bilious, and in excruciating pain, and all he could think about was the %$#& office holiday cards?

She ended the call quickly before snapping something ugly like, "I'm sorry if my gallbladder doesn't own a calendar."

She fumed all night. She had slaved for decades, and all he cared about was his blasted Christmas cards! How about a, "I'm sorry you feel bad, Rita." Or a, "Don't you worry about your job one bit—just focus on getting better."

After the surgery, while still groggy from anesthesia and pain medications, Rita was shocked to see her boss stroll into her hospital room carting a tiny bouquet of roses. Granted, they drooped and were tagged with a "Manager's Special: 50 percent off" sticker, but at least the cheapskate had made the effort to come visit her in the hospital! Maybe, beneath his crusty exterior, he really did care! She oohed and aahed over his half-wilted flowers and thanked him for coming.

He then pulled out a huge paper bag brimming with, you guessed it, Christmas cards, envelopes, addresses, and stamps, and flopped it onto her nightstand. "I figured while you were sitting around the hospital doing nothing, you could address these envelopes, stuff 'em, and put on the stamps. That way, we'll get these cards out in time." He seemed pleased with himself for coming up with a solution to the Christmas card dilemma.

Rita's mouth dropped. *Had he seriously just dumped four hundred Christmas cards on her nightstand just three hours after major surgery?*

Adding insult to injury he added, "Actually, Rita, the real reason I'm here is because no one else in the office knows the password to the computer. We couldn't schedule appointments today. Your surgery really fouled up my day."

"*Your day!* Try gallbladder surgery," she hissed under her breath.

He pulled out a notepad and pen and handed it to her. "Write down the passwords and the exact steps to get the computer working."

She stared at him, wanting to take his half-wilted, discount roses and his cumbersome bag of Christmas cards and clobber him over the head with them! For twenty-eight years, she had been the first one in the office and the last one to leave, so she'd always taken care of logging in and out of the computer. The other front desk assistant, while pleasant, was techno-challenged and never could remember how to log in. Thus, Rita had always just done it herself.

She gritted her teeth and gripped the bed rails. She had a good mind to write down the WRONG password and make him suffer for another day. Maybe for once, someone would appreciate all the work she did in that office!

She decided against such passive-aggressive behavior, however, because once she fully recovered from surgery, she would seek out a new job, and she'd need a glowing letter of recommendation from Dr. Frankel to land one. Time to get a life!

> *"Nothing else can substitute for a few well-chosen, well-timed, sincere words of praise. They're absolutely free—and worth a fortune."*
>
> ~SAM WALTON

Steak Knives and A-1 Sauce

Early in my practice, a medical-assistant student named Rhonda was assigned to our office for a one-month internship. She became the final straw in a long line of incompetent, loser students we'd endured over the years. First, she thought she was "above" filing charts. Her few attempts at blood drawing left large bruises on the patients' arms and no blood in the tubes. (Not that she was anyone to talk when it came to early attempts at learning blood drawing skills.) Furthermore, Rhonda insisted on taking her fifteen-minute smoke breaks twice a day at the exact time we were the busiest. Never mind we were overloaded with callbacks and behind schedule (because of her dreadful filing and phlebotomy skills, I might add)! Worse still, I learned after she left our office that she smoked more than cigarettes during her lunch breaks. Unbeknownst to me, she wore a roach clip on her belt to hold her joints. No wonder her filing was such a disaster. I'd falsely concluded she suffered from dyslexia.

One day, when every patient's urine dipstick showed massive amounts of blood, I became suspicious that Rhonda wasn't performing the test correctly. When I decided to observe her reading one, I discovered she was holding the dipstick *upside down*! This falsely made every patient urine sample looks like it was loaded with blood. Swell! Thus, I had to call every single patient and effectively say, "The good news? You don't have blood in your urine, and you can cancel your appointment with the urologist. The bad news? My medical-assistant student is a total moron!" (No, I didn't really say it, but I sure thought it!)

With time, we noticed the office prematurely ran out of pens and Post-it notes. Then postage stamps and rolls of toilet paper disappeared. Soon, hand sanitizer mysteriously vanished. When an electronic thermometer marched out of the office, I suspected our new student had kleptofingers, but I couldn't prove it.

The final straw? We had a luncheon scheduled with a pharmaceutical representative for the next day, so we circulated a menu around the office for each staff member to select a lunch item. We had an unspoken ten-dollar-per-employee price limit.

Imagine my shock when the office manager stormed into my office later that day and slammed the list of lunch items selected onto my desk. "Wait 'til you see this," she fumed.

I scanned the list and dropped my jaw. Rhonda had ordered herself a 16-ounce T-bone steak with a loaded baked potato, a large chicken Caesar salad, extra breadsticks, tortilla soup, fried mozzarella sticks, fruit tea, and cheesecake with extra strawberries. "This is just plain wrong," my office manager said, seething. "She's exploiting them!"

I scowled and shook my head in disgust. The girl had only worked with us for three weeks, and she had the nerve to order herself *sixty dollars'* worth of food for one lunch meal? I quickly tallied up the food items, and her choices added up to more than the rest of us combined!

"She needs a lesson in office etiquette," I said, handing the menu back to my office manager. "Change her order to a Junior-sized, plain hamburger. No fries. No pickle. No tomato. If she has the audacity to complain when the food arrives, tell her she can discuss it with me."

Rhonda had the audacity to show up for work the next day with a huge steak knife, a plastic bib, a bottle of A-1 steak sauce, and a large Tupperware to-go container for all her leftovers. When she opened her clamshell container and eyed only the lonely, small hamburger, she sputtered, "This isn't my order! I ordered steak. Where's my loaded potato? Where's my Caesar salad and breadsticks? And where's my cheesecake?" She glared at my office manager like she was the Grinch who stole Christmas.

Munching nonchalantly on a French fry, my office manager informed her of what I'd done and why.

With no remorse, Rhonda said, "My daddy always told me if someone offered to treat me to a meal, I should order the most expensive thing on the menu, including an appetizer, soup, salad, and dessert . . . and to ask for extra rolls."

Extra rolls, indeed! Perhaps Rhonda is more suited for a job with the federal government than a medical office!

"Good breeding consists of concealing how much we think of ourselves and how little we think of the other person."

~ MARK TWAIN

The Bedside Manner
of a Fence Post

Have you ever had a doctor who was book brilliant but bed-side-manner stupid? I've heard all kinds of horror stories over the years, like the surgeon who eyed one of my referred patients and snapped, "Why is every patient Dr. Burbank sends to me fat?"

One orthopedic kept a patient with excruciating back pain waiting for three hours, spent two seconds glancing at her MRI, then pronounced, "There's nothing I can do. Go home and live with it." He strutted out of the room, his consult over—except for his hefty three-hundred-dollar fee, that is.

Surgeons aren't the only ones who flunk Bedside Manner 101. Dr. Rood, a family practitioner, told a noncompliant blood pressure patient, "I don't give a %#@* if you take your blood pressure pill or not. I'm not the one who'll keel over dead or end up stroked out and in a nursing home." When another patient complained to him about her knee pain, he snapped, "That's what happens when you're older than the hills and big as a barn."

The worse bedside manner came from a cardiologist who treat-

"His final wish was that all his medical bills be paid promptly."

ed Alden Thurman. In fact, the doctor was so lacking in bedside manner, his wife called him "Dr. Doomsday" behind his back. At every office visit, he felt obligated to inform Alden that heart failure patients like him usually didn't survive more than five years; in short, he was living on borrowed time. One year, he admonished Alden with these uplifting words:

"Since you'll probably be dead by this time next year, be sure to finalize your will."

Still alive at ninety-three, more than fifteen years after his original diagnosis, Alden still plants a garden and mows the grass, thus defying Dr. Doomsday's dire predictions.

After Alden had a pacemaker inserted, his heart function improved significantly. While waiting for Dr. Doomsday to enter the exam room, Mrs. Thurman whispered to her husband, "Maybe since this last echocardiogram showed improved heart function, Dr. Doom and Gloom will give you a positive report for a change." (Dr. Doom and Gloom was her other pet name for the dour pessimist.)

No such luck! When he strolled into the exam room, he skimmed the echocardiogram report, grabbed a chair facing Mrs. Thurman, and completely ignored Alden. The first words out of his mouth? "Mrs. Thurman, if you walked into the kitchen and found your husband unarousable on the floor, what would you

do?"

Shocked that he'd ask such a blunt question right in front of her husband, she responded, "Well, I'd check his pulse and breathing, and if he didn't have any, I'd call 911 and initiate CPR using that new chest compression-only technique." She was proud of herself for remembering the new guidelines that no longer included mouth-to-mouth resuscitation.

"WRONG!" Dr. Doomsday bellowed. "*Don't* call 911. *Don't* start CPR. CALL THE MORGUE." He then launched into a dissertation on the dire outcomes of out-of-the-hospital CPR, and likely chances Alden would land in a permanent vegetative state if she attempted it. "Just leave him on the floor and call the morgue," Dr. Doomsday insisted.

Horrified, she replied, "Well, I wouldn't perform CPR if he were cold and stiff, but what if he had just barely keeled over? You want me to just leave him there and let him die?"

The doctor reiterated: "Unless you want to be married to a cucumber."

Alden, too stunned to say a word in the exam room, was quiet on the drive home. Finally, ever the tightwad, he asked his wife, "How much did I pay that fellow to tell you to call the morgue?"

Perhaps Alden—now ninety-four—will outlive the glum Doctor Doomsday yet! After all, laughter and a positive attitude make very good medicine!

"A cheerful heart is good medicine,
but a crushed spirit dries up the bones."

~ **Proverbs 17: 22** (NIV)

The Greatest Doctor in America

I recently received a letter from the "National Institute of Medicine" informing me I have been chosen for the Institute's prestigious "Award of Excellence." Despite not graduating from an Ivy League school, not publishing a single research paper, not graduating in the top 10 percent of my class, and not discovering a cure for cancer or a vaccine for AIDS, I am supposedly one of the nation's top internists.

"Congratulations!" you say? Not so fast! Apparently, my prodigious honor comes at a price: a mere five hundred dollars would buy me a lifetime membership into this esteemed society. For another ninety-nine dollars, they'll send me a lovely plaque to commemorate my distinguished status as a member of their elite society.

Right! If the Institute is so renowned and esteemed, how come I've never even *heard* of it? They are clearly trying to fool me into thinking they are the National Institutes of *Health*, which is highly esteemed.

Do they think I'm an idiot? If so, who ratted?

A while back, I received another letter congratulating me. Because of my supposed superior doctoring skills, I was chosen as "one of the top internists in the nation." My name would be listed in their lovely book, *Who's Who in Medicine*. If I wanted to obtain my own leather-bound special edition of this keepsake treasure to grace my coffee table and enjoy for years to come, I only had to fork out one hundred forty-nine dollars, plus fifteen bucks for shipping. Enjoy for years to come? *Do these people think I'd sit around reading the names of doctors for an evening's entertainment?*

Eight thousand idiots—excuse me, fellow doctors—had already been inducted into this joke of a medical society! I'll bet the publisher laughed his way to the bank and probably kept a copy of the book to know which doctors *not* to consult if he ever needed an intelligent doctor!

No doubt every doctor in the country received the exact same letter I did, and only those with ego issues or insomnia bought the dumb book. A more apt name for the book? *America's Dumbest Doctors.* Or better yet, *Who's Who in Gullible Doctors.*

"*A fool and his money are soon parted.*"

~ ENGLISH PROVERB

You Know You Have a Cheap HMO When...

- You request Viagra, but they mail you tongue depressors and duct tape instead.

- Your doctor moves into government-subsidized housing (the projects).

- Their idea of a cardiac stress test is your doctor performing a breast and abdominal exam with ice-cold hands.

SPONGE BATH? NO, BUT YOUR INSURANCE DOES COVER A SPONGE SHOWER...

- They turn down your request for a new allergy drug and instead mail you a pack of generic facial tissues with instructions for making nose plugs. They suggest giving your dog to a Vietnamese family.

- Your doctor submits a prior authorization for your gastric bypass surgery, but they turn it down and instead mail you a dog muzzle with threats that they'll triple your premium if you don't lose a hundred pounds by next year.

- The only specialists listed in their book have names you

can't spell or pronounce, and they obtained their medical degrees from sketchy institutions in Mongolia, or worse yet, online.

- Your doctor has more pending lawsuits than continuing education credits.

- The specialists listed to perform your colonoscopy are also listed in the Yellow Pages under "Mike's Rotor-Router Service."

- Your yearly physical is performed with you buck-naked because your doctor can no longer afford paper gowns.

- You wake up from anesthesia after major surgery sprawled face-first in the hospital parking lot.

- Your HMO is the only one the Department of Insurance has ever rated Z-minus.

- You call the Customer Complaint Department and after a forty-minute wait on hold, you are greeting with the following message: "Due to an unreasonable number of calls from whiny babies like you, we cannot answer your call right now. Leave your name and number, and we may, or may not, get back to you sometime within the next couple of months."

- Your labor is so painful you request an epidural. Instead, they bring a CD of breathing exercises and encouraging words such as, "You play, you pay!"

St. Peter at the Pearly Gates: *"What did you do to deserve entrance into heaven?"*

Dead Man: *"I was the CEO of the largest HMO in America."*

St Peter: *"Fine. You can enter—but only for three days."*

Every Bride's
Worst Nightmare

Like many women, Carrie had dreamed of her wedding day for years. At age thirty-three, she had strolled down more than her share of church aisles donning whatever gown the bride had selected for the bridesmaids. One dress had so many layers of frilly pink taffeta she felt more like an overgrown flower girl than an adult woman.

But that dress beat the garish fluorescent green number her brother's fiancé selected. It so glowed in the dark as she marched down the aisle that she wanted to leap under the pew.

The all-time worst dress, however, barely covered her tush, and it had such a low neckline she feared a wedding guest might catcall, or worse yet, slip her a fifty with a wink.

No way would she subject her friends to such humiliation! Her bridesmaids would don sophisticated and flattering black evening gowns. Adorned with a tasteful string of pearls, they would carry white calla lilies to match the pearls.

Carrie had already compiled a scrapbook full of wedding ideas when she finally met her Prince Charming. When he proposed, she hopped into action to make her dream wedding come true.

Her plans over the next six months progressed swimmingly, and to reward herself for all her hard work, she booked a suite at a Las Vegas hotel one week before the wedding. She and her three BFFs would enjoy a last-hurrah bachelorette bash, then they would fly back, and Carrie would have a full week to tie up all the last-minute details.

The four women had a wonderful time dancing, dining, catching Cirque du Soleil, and giggling long into the night. Carrie even managed to hit a minor jackpot and now returned to Nashville with more money than she'd taken.

She dragged her luggage into the Las Vegas airport with mixed emotions—sorry their weekend festivities were over but excited about her upcoming nuptials.

Since Southwest Airlines wouldn't grant specific seat assignments on her flight back to Nashville, Carrie was stuck sitting beside a grimy woman with mismatched clothes who smelled like she hadn't bathed in a month. Worse, the woman scratched at her scalp the entire trip. Carrie found out from the flight attendant that the plane held a huge group of refugees from Somalia, and unfortunately, because the plane was booked to capacity, she could not be moved to a less smelly seat.

As luck would have it, not only did the refugee carry body odor, she carried lice! I discovered this when Carrie showed up in my office three days before the wedding with an intensely itchy scalp and nits clinging stubbornly to nearly every strand of her long, thick hair. "You've got to do something," she said, clawing her scalp, eyes wide with worry. "I can't stand in a receiving line shaking hands and sharing hugs with three hundred guests when I'm infested with lice!" She shook her head in despair. "I'll need to add a bottle of 'Lice-B-Gone' shampoo to my gift bags!" She grabbed my arm and beseeched me, "Please, help me!"

I instructed Carrie in the proper use of a "nit comb" and prescribed a strong shampoo for killing lice. (I then made a hasty exit from the exam room, changed my lab coat, scrubbed my hands until they were raw, and prayed I wouldn't contract the itchy little devils!)

Unfortunately, she was back two days later, now hysterical. "The wedding is tomorrow, and I'm still infested."

A quick glance at her black tresses confirmed the stubborn refugee vermin had found a happy home on Carrie's scalp!

"At this rate, I'm gonna spend my entire honeymoon picking nits."

Worse still, while in my office, Carrie received a phone call from a very upset bridesmaid—she and another bridesmaid had contracted lice as well!

Carrie dropped her head into her hands. Here she had chosen *evening black* for her bridesmaid dresses because she thought that would whisper "sophistication." Now, every nit and louse would stand out against the black material, and her bridesmaids would look like low-class trailer trash.

"This wedding has turned into a disaster!" exclaimed Carrie. "Do I need to call the whole thing off? Is this an omen I'm not meant to marry Wayne?"

After I calmed Carrie down, my nurse painstakingly combed Carrie's hair strand-by-strand with the nit comb until every single nit had been removed. We then sent her home to wash her hair *again* with the potent lice shampoo. I instructed Carrie to have her bridesmaids do the same. I crossed my fingers and hoped for the best.

Carrie moved out of state immediately after the wedding, so I never did hear if the bride and bridesmaids walked down the aisle lice-free or not, but on a positive note, the calla lilies looked lovely!

Dedication

My Greatest Regret

We met in Sunday school ten years ago. Never mind he was over eighty, and I was forty-three. Whether debating biblical principles or politics, Jack and I clicked. I was the supposed leader of our class, but he was the heart and soul. His humor, practical wisdom, and kindness endeared him to everyone in the class. When Jack shared his own struggles and temptations, he opened the door for the rest of us to expose our dark sides and worries. When I requested his prayers in locating a medical partner to join my practice, he told me he'd already been praying for me every day for weeks now. *Every day for weeks?* How many people in my life had cared enough to sacrifice precious time every single day to pray for me? I felt humbled and loved beyond measure.

Jack's sacrificial love didn't end with prayer, though. As a thank-you for teaching the class, he gave me a beautiful Chinese wisteria from a top nursery in McMinnville because I once mentioned how much I loved inhaling the fragrance of my neighbor's wisteria. He always thanked me for a great lesson, even when I knew it was mediocre. He arrived early every Sunday to prepare piping hot coffee and to greet the early birds and new members.

He might have been eighty-four years old and unable to perform cartwheels, but Jack was our cheerleader. Whether I had published a magazine article, lost five pounds, or cultivated a gorgeous dinner-plate dahlia, Jack believed in me, encouraged me, advised me, and became my Nashville surrogate father. Soon, his wife, son, and daughter-in-law became like family to me as well.

One night Jack and his wife attended my husband's WannaBeatles rock concert. Picture a slightly stooped octogenarian with a hearing aid and tremor rocking out to "Back in the U.S.S.R." After the concert, Jack complimented the electric guitarist for nailing an intricate riff. Earlier that year he attended my daughter's harp debut and my husband's pipe organ concert, despite claiming to be nearly tone-deaf.

In short, I learned how to love others through Jack's example: investing time to pray when he might rather read a book, attending another's play or concert, choosing the perfect gift, offering praise and encouragement.

Unfortunately, Jack developed terminal cancer, and our roles reversed. Now I was the one praying daily for a miracle. I completed a Med-line computer search hoping for a research trial or treatment somewhere that would cure him. But none of the currently available treatments offered a cure. Thus, I visited him in the hospital with a bouquet of my dinner-plate dahlias and offered medical advice to his sons. I whipped up a meal, including my much-acclaimed strawberry trifle.

Whether I wanted to admit it or not, Jack was dying. He lost weight and became so weak he could no longer attend Sunday school. Before long, hospice nurses intervened with morphine.

While I e-mailed and called regularly, I couldn't bear to see him bed-bound, so thin and incoherent. I wanted to remember him the way he used to be before cancer and morphine drips . . . before the greedy eyes of death taunted me and that emperor of all maladies sucked the life out of the godliest man I knew.

What was there about dying people and death that made me so uncomfortable? Truth be told, I'd rather tour a nuclear dump than stare into a coffin at a dead body at a funeral or small talk at calling hours. Shouldn't I be comfortable with death and dying by now? I'd read all the books and ushered more than a few patients onto the other side in my twenty years as a doctor, but it never got easier.

As a Christian, I should be filled with joy at how Jack would soon walk the golden streets of heaven, free of cancer and pain. Instead, I dreaded losing my dear friend and mentor and didn't want to face it. Praying for a miracle seemed less painful than facing his death head on. I couldn't do it. It was too depressing, too morbid, and too awkward.

You should visit him, my conscience nagged, but fear eroded my courage. What would I say? "How are you doing, Jack?" Duh! He's dying and hooked up to morphine! How do you *think* he's doing? Okay, how about, "I'm praying for a miracle." We both knew God was choosing not to answer this prayer with a miracle, so I'd just be rubbing it in. What about, "I'll see you on the other side!" Definitely not! Trite. Impertinent. I sighed, clueless of what to say or how to act.

I imagined myself standing at his bedside, stiff as a telephone pole, trying to dig up something, anything, meaningful to say, both of us heaving a giant sigh of relief when I left, and the awkward encounter ended. Some professional I was—I dreaded death more than the Ebola virus and AIDS combined.

What I wanted to say was, "Jack, seeing you so thin and frail and suffering like this breaks my heart. You've been such a blessing to my family and me. I'll miss you so much. Please don't die, 'cause we need you down here."

If I spilled out my heart like a rupturing aneurysm, would I break down, sob, weep, and carry on, clutching his arm and begging him not to die? Worse yet, if I fell apart and told him how much he'd meant to me, how much I loved him, would his wife get the wrong impression and think something tawdry or inappropriate had gone on between us? That would be terrible! What if I became so overcome with grief he and his wife ended up consoling *me*, instead of me comforting *them*? Just what they needed—me falling apart at the seams.

So I didn't go. For *their* sakes, I told myself. I chickened out and listened to the voice of fear.

Now I wish I'd told him how much his unconditional love

and encouragement had meant to me. How his corny jokes and funny stories made me laugh. How I respected his wisdom and spiritual insights. How I loved his gardening tips and his Big Boy tomatoes. How I would miss our discussions about books and our debates about world affairs.

I wish I'd told him how he had taught me to love others through his Christ-like example. How he'd blessed my family and our entire Sunday school class.

I wish I'd told him how much we all would miss him.

But I didn't. Because it might become too emotional, too sad, or too awkward.

Jack, if you can read this in heaven, please forgive me and know how much I loved you. I'm sorry I abandoned you when you needed me most, but I know you have already forgiven me, because that's the kind of person you are.

Reader, tell your anchors and kindred spirits how much they mean to you before it's too late. If you can't muster the courage to do it eyeball-to-eyeball, write a letter. Find some way to let them know. Don't let them die without your words of gratitude and love. Learn from my mistake, because I've learned the hard way there is something far worse than awkwardness: regret.

This book is dedicated to the memory of William Jack Casteel, who suggested I write a book about my doctoring experiences. I will never forget his kindness and godly example. He was a blessing to everyone who knew him and is still dearly missed.

"Lead your life so you wouldn't be ashamed to sell the family parrot to the town gossip."

~ **WILL ROGERS**

I am grateful for the expertise of Larry Carpenter and his team at Clovercroft in orchestrating the production of this book. Lorraine Bossé-Smith's content editing fine-tuned my writing skills, and Suzanne Lawing's talent at cover design and internal formatting added a playful but professional look. Her creativity is amazing! Gail Fallen performed the thankless but necessary job of proofreading with finesse.

Kudos to Theresa McCracken (McHumor) and P.C. Vey for designing five of the cartoons used to illustrate this book. Thank you, John Simmons of Cartoon Stock, for assisting me in locating the home of many of these cartoons when I was ready to pull my hair out!

Dorothy Willard (my wonderful mother), Eliza Burbank (my brilliant daughter), and Nathan Burbank (my long-suffering husband) all assisted with editing and critiquing my stories. Most of the time I was grateful for their blunt honesty!

Judy Dowlen worked tirelessly with me to dig up the many quotations used to spice up each story. Judy's bubbly encouragement and support when I felt overwhelmed buoyed me to the finish line.

My poor husband and children endured manuscripts, cartoons, quotes, and a general avalanche of paper scattered throughout the house for months as I tried to pull together all the elements of this book. Even my in-laws, John and Lois Burbank, were roped into this project! I love you all dearly!

Lastly, I'd like to thank all of the wonderful patients who have trusted me with their health care over the years. After doctoring you for over twenty years, some of you seem like family to me! My life is so much richer because of you, and I thank you for your friendship and the many lessons learned from you!

CARTOON RIGHTS

About the Author

SALLY WILLARD BURBANK started life on a small dairy farm in northern Vermont. She graduated summa cum laude from Texas Christian University then completed her medical training at the University of Vermont College of Medicine. After marrying her longtime sweetie, Nathan, they moved to Nashville, Tennessee, to complete her internship  and residency training. She has practiced internal medicine in Nashville since 1986.

The proud mother of two college students, she enjoys gardening, reading, bicycling, cooking, and catering to the whims of a yappy but adorable silky terrier named Tiger Lily. She does not enjoy working out on her elliptical, but does it anyway to keep up with her love of all things chocolate.

She has published multiple stories in *Chicken Soup for the Soul, Angels on Earth* magazine, and several anthologies. She co-leads Nashville Christian Writers and is a member of American Christian Fiction Writers and Romance Writers of America. She has written two novels, which she hopes to publish soon!

Check out her author's page on Facebook, and keep abreast of her zany patients by reading her blog:

www.patientswewillneverforget.wordpress.com

*An autographed copy of this book may be
purchased directly from the author by mailing
a check for twenty dollars to:*

Patients I Will Never Forget
207 Woodmont Circle
Nashville, TN 37205

Make check payable to Sally Burbank.